Growing Better Roses

Fred J. Nisbet

Growing Better Roses

ETCHINGS BY THOMAS O'DONOHUE

ALFRED A. KNOPF   NEW YORK   1974

THIS IS A BORZOI BOOK
PUBLISHED BY ALFRED A. KNOPF, INC.

Library of Congress Cataloging in Publication Data
Nisbet, Fred J   (date)   Growing better roses.
Bibliography: p.
1. Rose culture.   2. Roses—Varieties.
I. Title.
SB411.N58   1974   635'.933'72   73–7300
ISBN 0–394–48538–6

Manufactured in the United States of America
First Edition

To Shirley, my wife,

whose encouragement and understanding
made this book possible

Contents

Introduction

It is now easier to grow better roses than ever before. Roses, long everybody's favorite flower, have had a reputation for most of this century—if not longer—for being hard to grow. Much of this reputation was deserved, although some of this fault lay with the gardener himself—and not with the roses. But gardening has made tremendous strides in recent years, especially in rose growing. The only trouble is that many gardeners don't realize this.

Roses are no longer hard to grow! If you don't believe me, just consider these recent changes:

Item 1. Rose breeders have changed their priorities and methods. Now they look first for a vigorous plant, with attractive, *disease-resistant* foliage. Next, they look for new or better coloring of well-shaped blooms, and plenty of them. Fragrance is given a higher rating than previously; it is even planned for in making crosses. More rigorous testing for wide adaptability and hardiness tops off all good breeding programs. By having better plants to grow, how can you lose?

Item 2. Although we haven't made much progress in handling soils, at least at the amateur gardener's level, new methods and materials in fertilization are, actually, revolutionary! It is no longer "feast or famine," and we keep them growing—and *blooming*—all season long. This builds stronger plants, which survive the winter's cold better than previously.

Item 3. The rootstocks on which the cultivars (horticultural varieties, ones that have originated and persisted under cultivation) used to be budded were a mixed, seedling lot, and the results were as varied. Now really good strains of *Rosa multiflora* and Dr. Huey give uniformity and good results in most of the country. Special kinds are available for the semitropical areas, so that there roses are no longer "annuals" but true, long-lived shrubs.

Item 4. At long last we have learned the utter folly of "hard pruning"—where only about three canes were allowed to grow, and these were cut back to three or four eyes. This was rationalized as the way to "produce large blooms on long stems," which was the result—as long as the tortured plants survived! This was far too short a time, however, and winter casualties were horrendous—for the plants never had any chance to build up any reserves of strength. Now, with light to moderate pruning, rose plants are treated as hardy shrubs, not as bedding plants. They grow better, produce more blooms, and live far longer as a result.

Item 5. Except for the "once over lightly" spring cleanup, the *hoe is dead!* That hot, sweaty, dusty chore of maintaining a "dust mulch" during the dry periods of the summer is a thing of the past. Now, just as soon as the rose beds are really clean in the spring, when pruning and fertilizing are finished, a mulch is applied. This not only keeps down most weeds, it conserves moisture (leading to more even growth) and improves the soil structure. Most mulches also add considerable humus to the soil as well. When you improve growth while greatly reducing labor, that's *real* progress!

Item 6. The greatest single change in rose growing in decades lies in the field of pesticides. The development of benomyl (Benlate, and so on) has reduced the heaviest of all work loads of rose growing—prevention of diseases—by as much as *two-thirds*. Instead of having to spray every week from first leaf development until final leaf drop (too many months, regardless of where you garden) spraying is now on a once-every-two- (or even *three*-) weeks basis. You can now take a good vacation without feeling guilty!

As for insecticides, the newer "broad spectrum" kinds do a wonderful job on many kinds of pests at once; special formulations, however, are still required for thrips, borers, and bad infestations of mites. Unlike the fungicides, these materials need to be used only when the pests are "in residence"; with the present concern for a clean environment, it is normal today to avoid "multipurpose" sprays and use only what is actually needed at the moment. This reduces costs, too.

Item 7. If the above is not enough to inspire thousands of gardeners to grow roses, consider this: for anyone who grows more than a couple of dozen rose plants, a revolutionary new tool is now just becoming available, one that not only reduces the time and effort required for a good job, but cuts material costs (and with benomyl this can be substantial) by as much as three-quarters and results in better plant growth! This paragon is a small "mist blower," electrically operated and carried on an over-the-shoulder strap. It sends an extremely fine fog of pesticides (and fertilizers, if desired) swirling over *all surfaces* of the plants. This totally enveloping mist is said to give better pest control than has ever been achieved before—even with the reduced labor and materials. Time is also saved, in major amounts.

Item 8. Finally, winter protection is being improved, although not at the rate of most of the above procedures. The new plastic "shells" are reducing labor and increasing livability somewhat—so that is at least some progress. (This factor, of course, is only of any considerable importance to the gardeners in the really cold parts of the country.)

THE TOTAL PICTURE

With modern rose plants greatly improved and just about every growing operation made easier and more effective as well, it seems time for everyone to grow roses—few or many. If you have the room and the desire, grow a hundred or more. If you have to settle for five Miniatures on a window sill, you will enjoy that, too.

In any event, grow some roses—and have fun!

Growing Better Roses

Chapter 1

Siting the Garden

Most gardeners do not have much control over where they grow their plants. There are, however, some considerations that must be observed if you are to have a good chance of success.

CLIMATE

This most stringent of all factors can put a definite limit on what should be attempted, at least at its northern (or high elevation) extremes. A proper selection of the cultivars or species to be grown and a well-devised winter protection program will make it possible to grow roses in just about the most severe sections of the country. On the other hand, in subtropical regions it is now possible, by the proper selection of rootstocks and by using the cultural methods peculiar to such areas, to grow fine roses where failure was common just a few years ago.

No one in his right mind, for example, would try to grow some of the more tender (true) Tea roses in Rochester, New York, or in Saint Paul. Yet the hardier cultivars among the Hybrid Teas, Floribundas, and Grandifloras will grow beautifully in those places, if given good winter protection. Of course, many of the species, shrub, and Old roses can fill out many a garden in such areas. It is important to select only the hardiest of each of these groups for such locations.

The "Proof of the Pudding" ratings of the American Rose Society, which rates hundreds of kinds of roses for many qualities, are a big help here. Your local nurseryman and members of your local rose society will have more helpful suggestions.

A NOTE ON HARDINESS

The hardiness of any species or cultivar is a constant factor, regardless of where it is grown. Don't avoid roses grown in Texas, California, or Oregon just because you garden in Duluth. If a cultivar is hardy in Saint Johnsbury, Vermont, you can buy it from any source and it will still be hardy there.

LIGHT

The rule of thumb is that roses need at least six hours of sunlight each day if they are to do well. If an ideal condition exists, it is where the sunlight comes into the garden early, drying the foliage quickly, reducing the incidence of disease. Then, during the heat of the afternoon, a light shade is beneficial: the blooms fade less and last longer.

There is a bit of leeway here, but not much. While full sunlight is desired, if there is enough good indirect light to piece out a slight shortage of direct sunlight, quite good results can be obtained.

The Musk roses will make good growth with less direct sunlight than almost

A good place to study rose growing is in an established rose garden,
such as this one in Longwood Gardens, Kennett Square, Pennsylvania.
Here you can learn the different classes,
how they are used, and then the different cultivars.

any other kind, and some of them, especially in the newer cultivars such as Will Scarlet, are very nice roses indeed.

AIR

Areas in which there is not a good, "normal" flow of air are not for roses; in stagnant areas diseases become almost insurmountable.

And on the other hand, windswept locations are almost as bad. But at least here it is possible to temper the wind in many cases, and this is all that is necessary. A hedge to the windward side, not close enough to give root competition, will generally be all that is required. Where there is not room for that, a fence will do, *if it is not a tight surface;* this will do more damage than good. A "semisolid" fence will slow the wind down to reasonable proportions and the plants will grow. A solid fence or wall will swirl the wind—of increased velocity—around the plants and ruin them.

ROOT COMPETITION

Roses will tolerate less root competition than many other plants, especially from trees; it is practically impossible to supply enough nutrients and water for them both. Such surface-rooting trees as maples and elms and such shrubs as yews do not make good neighbors. Deep, tap-rooted plants, such as oaks, are not as bad, but even they should not come too close.

Where plantings have to be too close together, because of space limitations, there is a way out. Dig a narrow trench at the edge of the rose bed 26 inches deep. Lay sheets of corrugated aluminum roofing (they are 22 inches wide and come in various lengths—fit length to the size of the bed) *on edge* in the trench and fill in. Such a barrier should last for years.

SOIL AND ITS AMENDMENTS

The "ideal rose soil" is a good loam, well supplied with humus, that is well drained and has a pH between 5.5 and 6.5 (slightly acid). This is what gardeners dream of, but all too many of them have to make do with soils that are a considerable distance from this ideal—on either the light or heavy side.

It is fortunate for us that roses are really rather adaptable as far as the soil is concerned. Quite good results can be gained on many soils—short of the very sandy and the almost pure clays.

A "good loam" is made up, from the mineral standpoint, of from 35 to 50 percent sand, with some silt and some clay. Added to this there must be a considerable amount of humus, a decay product of organic matter.

If your soil varies far from this, there are ways of improving it.

Sand and Clay

Clay is cheap but it is heavy, and it takes a great deal of labor to spread it over a too-light soil and work it in evenly. Only on excessively sandy soils is it practical to add clay, except in small amounts.

Sand, on the other hand, is easier to handle, and it may be used to lighten pure clay soils—in moderation, for it takes an unbelievable amount to do the whole job.

In cases where the mineral imbalance in the soil is not extreme, sand and clay are generally disregarded, and organic elements are used to achieve a balanced soil.

Organic Matter and Humus

No sandy soil, or one of almost pure clay, can become a good loam without humus. As organic matter breaks down, it releases the elements from which it was built.

More important, some of these elements form "humic acids," usually called "humus." These gummy materials work magic on soils, bringing sand particles into clumps called "crumb structure," which is the basis of fine loams. This same humus also serves to break up the most solid clays, making them warmer, able to drain better, and much easier to work, and giving them a more open structure for gaseous exchange in the soil atmosphere.

As organic matter is so important, what sources are best? Any decision on this point must be decided, to some extent, on your local conditions.

First, determine the relative values and drawbacks of the various sources. Then you can check to find which are *regularly* available locally and are reasonable in price.

ANIMAL MANURES

The first major source of organic matter is animal manures, prized for their improvement of soils, even good loams. They should be mixed with "litter" (hay, straw, leaves, wood chips, or the like) and be well rotted. Horse manure, when fresh, can burn badly, but cow manure is cold; the latter, however, ruins soil structure when used fresh. Chicken manure burns severely when fresh, so it should be well mixed with litter and composted for a time; it does less for the soil structure than any other manure, except possibly guano. (Dog manures contain toxic acids and should never be used around plants!)

First choice among rose growers seems to be cow manure (steer in the Southwest), and it should be used where it is available and the price isn't outrageous—which is the common situation today, especially in cities.

These manures add much to the soil beyond the humus value—beneficial bacteria, some hormones, and microfertilizing elements, especially. Do not, however, depend upon manures to supply much to the general fertility picture; not only are the major elements in low supply, they are not even in balanced supply. Limit the use of manures on very heavy clays, as excessive amounts can lead to problems.

There is one place where animal manures should not be used. Where either the soil or the irrigation water is very alkaline, to a point where it is difficult to keep a pH reading of 7.0 or less, forget manures.

PEAT MOSS

The second major source of organic matter is peat moss. There is a trap here. Some bagged or bulk *peat* is made up of nearly decomposed sedges. This material has its uses, but not for our purposes; it will not hold its structure for any length of time. Peat *moss* is derived from sphagnum moss; its structure will hold for a long time, and when it does break down it adds some little fertility to the soil.

You have some control over the rate of breakdown—in the grade you buy. The usual "horticultural grade" is medium in texture, but the grade used by poultry farmers as litter is appreciably coarser, so it takes longer to disintegrate (it may often be cheaper, too). Peat moss is widely available, the cost is not too bad, and, if you stick to one good brand, you can be assured of uniformity—which is rare in the organic field.

COMPOST

The third member of the organic-matter triumvirate is compost—pure gold for any gardener. This you can—and should—make for yourself. It has some small amount of fertility (depending on what goes into it), but it is like manures in that it contains beneficial bacteria, possibly some hormones, possibly some trace elements, and *lots* of humus. Good gardeners have two compost piles or bins, at the very least—one for current use and the other(s) "working."

Simply stated, making compost is like making a layer cake. About six inches of "organic matter" is laid down. This may be lawn clippings, leaves, vegetable skins or refuse from the kitchen, weeds from the garden (which have not gone to seed), or whatever. Even small amounts of shredded newspaper can be used. Just be certain that the material is clean—that is, that it is not contaminated with diseases, insects, or, again, weed seeds. Scatter on this a liberal dusting of treble super-phosphate (and if your soil test showed the need, some agricultural limestone). Now add a two-inch layer of good soil—plus an inch or so of manure, if you have it. Repeat the process until the stack is as high as you can work easily. Make your stack straight sided and make the top dish-shaped, so that rain will trickle through the stack, rather than run off; if necessary, water the stack during dry weather, but don't ever let it get soggy!

When the stack has developed some heat and then cooled, break it up, starting at the top and working down, and make a new stack alongside, mixing the materials thoroughly as you do. When this has "worked," you should have some first-rate compost. The time required, of course, depends on the season.

"Compost activators" are widely advertised "to speed up the decomposition and add valuable nutrients." Where manure is used or where the soil is of really good quality they are not necessary, although they *may* speed up the process somewhat; with no manure and poor soil they can help.

OTHER GOOD SOURCES

There are other sources of organic matter that are often used, generally because they are locally plentiful and inexpensive. Chief among these would be well-rotted *coarse* or *medium* sawdust (fine sawdust is a liability, not an asset). Wood chips and shredded bark are now becoming widely available. Unless they have been treated with some fertilizer, they should have some ammonium sulfate or other nitrogen source added, and should be composted for about three months before they are used. An identical treatment should be used for wood shavings, which are of less value.

Leaves are commonly available, but care should rule here. Stiff, brittle leaves, such as those from oaks or beeches, are good, especially if they are composted a bit before using. Soft leaves, as those from maples and birches, get wet and form impenetrable masses, which can actually suffocate plant roots; thorough composting is necessary if they are to be used at all.

Lawn clippings are often mentioned as a source of organic matter. Unless they are well composted, however, don't use them, for they give rise to molds and can mat as badly as maple leaves. Hay and straw, which need some composting, are not good sources, as they are invariably extremely good sources, in their turn, of weed seeds. If you can get soybean or alfalfa hay cheap (generally because it is moldy, which doesn't hurt), by all means use it; it contains a fairly good amount of nitrogen.

Such offbeat sources as seaweed (must be composted), cotton and peanut hulls, and cotton and tobacco waste and stems can be used—where available. Ground corncobs are of less use here than as a mulch; but they can be used in a pinch, if nitrogen is added to aid in the breakdown. Buckwheat hulls break down far too slowly to be of any value.

Both lime (alkaline) and gypsum (neutral), sometimes called land plaster, help greatly in making heavy clays more open and friable. Which you use will depend on the normal pH of your soil.

If you can't afford a layout like this, at least you can steal design ideas.
Here the roses tie the whole design together—they form a theme.
The use of water, a few boxwoods for contrast,
and the sculptured finials and pottery all add strength
to the design. The use of a few Climbers would help greatly.

WATER

Roses need considerable water at all times if they are to grow and bloom well. But—they must have it on their own terms!

The usual rule-of-thumb says that one inch is needed every week of the growing season and that the soil should never get really dry in the winter. This is a good start—for *average conditions.* For very light soils, and where the climate is hot and dry, double this amount can often be used to advantage. And where the soil is very heavy, especially in mild or cool climates, this might be reduced by 25 percent, more or less.

The truth is, we don't know very much about water relationships for most ornamental plants—so experiment in your garden to see what your plants really need. To keep them growing *uninterruptedly* is your goal, and they won't do that if they are short of water.

WATERING EQUIPMENT

The usual sprinklers are of no use in the rose garden; they wet the leaves, and that encourages the growth of diseases.

For small plantings, a semiporous canvas hose can be wound around the plants; this is a slow process, and the hose must be repositioned from time to time until all plants have been watered. Faster is the flat plastic hose with small holes on one surface. This can be used if the holes are placed in contact with the soil; it is faster, but must still be repositioned from time to time.

The "spaghetti type" watering devices are nothing but a hose connection hooked up to (usually) six small hoses of graduated lengths. One hose end is placed at the base of each plant; when the watering is done, the device is moved to another group of plants. This is even faster than the previously mentioned device, but still requires moving each time six plants are watered.

A major breakthrough has just been made in this field with the introduction of a "microporous" plastic pipe, which seems to have everything. This pipe, which oozes water uniformly throughout its whole length, is buried about eight inches deep between two rows of plants, a process that does not involve much labor, as the trench is quite narrow. This means that the water is delivered *in the soil* at the root zone—and there is no waste. Users find that growth is very strong and that the incidence of disease is reduced. After the system is installed, the only labor is turning the water on and off, no matter how many plants are being grown. If these initial findings prove to be universal, this could be *the* system of the future!

DRAINAGE

The negative aspect of water shows in areas where the drainage is poor. Roses can't stand "wet feet."

If your soil is heavy, don't just dig a deep hole, put some gravel in the bottom, and then plant. What this does is create a "bathtub": water from the surrounding soil will drain into it and make matters worse, rather than better. First, probe the area two feet deep with a crowbar, soil auger or post-hole digger. If an impervious layer (hardpan) is located, break it up by puncturing it, at one-foot intervals over the whole area involved, with a crowbar. Another way to assess the drainage is to clock the time needed for all water to drain from the area after a heavy rain. If some spots are slow, make tests, by boring, to see why. If no hardpan is encountered and yet the drainage is slow, install tile drains, two and a half to three feet deep, and connect them to a sewage system or run them to a lower point for discharge. If more serious problems are encountered, see your county agricultural agent or check with the agricultural engineering department of your state university for help.

Chapter 2

The First Decisions

There is one question that alone can determine whether you will enjoy growing roses or give up in disgust. That is—how many will you grow?

If you let your enthusiasm get away from you and try too many, you will have neither good roses nor any fun! If, on the other hand, you are realistic in your estimates of the amount of work involved and then plant 10 to 15 percent fewer plants than you think you can handle, the whole project should go well and be a real joy. You won't always have that rushed feeling; you can sit back often and enjoy the beauty you have created.

Ten roses well cared for can give wonderful satisfaction. Twenty poorly cared for will be a disappointment. It's as simple as that!

If you aren't certain of your estimate of the work involved, *be pessimistic*—for the first year, anyway. At the end of the first year it will be easy to enlarge your plantings. Where too large a garden has resulted in poor growth, it is difficult to reduce a planting and try to revive the remaining weakened plants.

Don't forget: if all your other decisions are right but you make a mistake on this one, then the end result will be failure. So plan small—just this once—and enjoy yourself.

LABOR SAVING THROUGH DESIGN

Now that you know how many plants you will have and where they will be, you can plan your garden. Much labor can be saved by proper planning. Whether the garden is formal or informal, simplicity is a virtue.

Make walks wide enough so that any equipment can be handled with ease. Those surfaced with brick or gravel are usable more of the time than grass. Turf walks at the edge of beds, as well as lawns, require regular edging, a tiresome task, and hand trimming of the edge is generally required after each mowing. Where the beds are edged with brick, laid flat, most of these chores are eliminated. This strip will also prevent grasses, especially such an invasive grass as Bermuda, from growing into the beds.

Edgings of dwarf boxwood look fine in formal settings, but they require extra care to keep them trim and healthy.

More and more rose growers are adding a wall, six inches or more high, inside the "mowing strip." This may be made of brick, stone, railroad ties, or even cut sheets of Transite. It helps drainage, where that is marginal, prevents runoff when watering, and keeps the mulch in place. Along the Gulf Coast, in Florida and other places where the water table is high, this is a must.

Formal gardens have an advantage in that the roses are kept together. In informal plantings, such as mixed borders, the work load is greater.

When a rose bed can be approached from front and back, three rows can be

All the elements of good design are here.
Note good background, use of water, statuary,
and ample width of walks, among other ideas.
On a smaller scale this would still be lovely.

This very simple yet very pleasing design
can be duplicated on a reduced scale
on almost any
nonlevel suburban lot.

cared for without actually getting into the bed to any great extent. Where you can get to the plants from only one side, two rows is the practical limit. If the beds have to be deeper than this, allow a wider spacing every three rows, so there will be a narrow path to work from without getting torn by thorns. This should be a minimum of 14 inches when the plants are *fully grown*.

PROPER SPACING

How far apart the plants should be depends on two main factors—the kind of rose and where it is grown.

Where Hybrid Teas are grown under severe climatic conditions (Concord, New Hampshire, Saint Paul, and so on) a *minimum* of two feet is about right, for growth here is not great. In moderate climates (Philadelphia, Seattle, and so on), the plants grow longer, so two and a half feet is minimum. In mild areas (Savannah, Houston, Santa Barbara, and so on), increase to three feet. All of these are minimums, so add six to nine inches where especially good growth comes from either very vigorous cultivars or your superior growing of the plants.

Generally speaking, these distances are suitable for Floribundas, especially strong-growing kinds, such as Frensham; light-growing kinds, such as Gold Cup, may be planted a bit closer. Polyanthas can be planted as close as 18 inches in severe climates, and seldom need more than two feet in milder climates.

Grandifloras generally fit the spacing for Hybrid Teas, although some of the more vigorous can stand an added six inches.

It is difficult to categorize the Old roses, but three to three and a half feet should be the least dimension; this is about right for the strongest of the Hybrid Perpetuals, although most of them (such as General Jacqueminot, Henry Nevard, or Mrs. John Laing) fit the pattern of Hybrid Teas very well.

Climbing Hybrid Teas seldom need more than six feet, but most Large-Flowered Climbers, unless pruned severely, need about eight. A few very robust kinds, such as Mermaid, need 12 feet or more.

Tree roses are generally spaced five to six feet apart, but in those few areas where these really take off, such as San Francisco, eight feet is better.

By all means, do not crowd your plantings! The plants will not grow as well when crowded, pest control and pruning are made more difficult, and foliage will become badly scarred from the thorns of neighboring plants.

On the other hand, if you are very short of space you can increase the number of plants in a given space by staggering the rows; this will gain about six to nine inches per plant.

At this point you may find it advisable to adjust the number of plants you are planning on growing to fit the available room.

PLANNING ON PAPER

Put your plan *on paper!* Even if the draughtsmanship is rough, mark the location of each plant and the name of the plant destined to grow in that location. Spend a bit of time selecting the color sequences in each bed. Some of the new "fluorescent reds" simply kill such lovely pinks as Queen Elizabeth. In fact, they are better grown in a bed of their own—if you can manage it—preferably next to a good white.

When you are ready to plant, this advance planning will really pay off, for you will know exactly what you must do next. (In the raw, damp chill of spring planting, this is an item of merit!)

A further note: Neatly executed scale drawings on good tracing paper look mighty impressive on the dining room table or your desk in the study, but they are not too practical to work with. A better solution would be to use a sawyer's broad-stroke pencil on big sheets of heavy butcher's paper and to draw to a large, easily read scale. This can be laid on the ground by the edge of the bed, held in place by a few rocks or bricks, and read easily and quickly when planting time arrives.

Chapter 3

Buying Good Plants and Planting Them Properly

WHERE TO BUY PLANTS

Many gardeners live near one or more good nurseries, so those are the logical places to start, especially if roses are featured. There you can get much helpful advice, not only on growing techniques, but also on what cultivars do especially well in your area—useful information seldom available at the nursery counters of supermarkets, hardware or chain stores. Most good nurseries, too, carry only the top grade of roses, while this is rare with the nonnursery outlets. And in addition the nurseryman has the knowledge and facilities for keeping his plants in top shape. Nonnursery outlets seldom have either.

There are many mail-order nurseries which cater to those gardeners who live far from a nursery. Some of these specialize in roses, or at least feature them. Gardeners who have a fairly large collection often find that such outfits can supply cultivars not available locally. And with the improved packing methods now used by the better mail-order houses, roses can be delivered in first-class shape anywhere.

Again it should be stressed that the climate in which a rose is grown has no bearing on its inherent hardiness. There is, however, one situation in which growers in very severe climates should stick to northern-grown plants. When planting in the fall, it is usual to try to have six weeks of establishment time before freeze-up. This places the planting date so early in the really cold areas that southern roses are not yet available, as they have not fully hardened for the winter. By spring planting time this particular problem has disappeared; in any case, fall planting in such areas is taking an unnecessary risk (see page 33 for a further discussion of this point).

WHICH ROOTSTOCK?

Getting the right rootstock on rose bushes used to be pretty much a question of luck, unless you could get cultivars budded on *Rosa canina*, the English Dog rose. Even the early use of *R. multiflora* wasn't always successful, as seedlings from very mixed batches of seed were used.

Today, *R. multiflora* is very widely used, and the resulting plants grow vigorously and hardily over a wide range of conditions, from the Far North to most of the South. The difference lies in the fact that modern "multiflora" may be any one of scores of *selected* strains or clones, the result of decades of rigorous selection on the part of the rose nurserymen.

Another fine rootstock, used very widely in the huge California growing fields, is Dr. Huey, sometimes called Shafter. This kind is also vigorous, hardy, and very adaptable.

These two modern stocks take care of most of the country (check with your dealer which is used), but the semitropical section of the South is a different propo-

Circular gardens are a relief from the more usual squares and rectangles.
The statuary is distinctive and pleasing.
But the design almost falls apart, as the beds are
too narrow to stand alone without a background.

sition. Most modern varieties grown near Tampa, for example, and budded on multiflora, are very short lived, far from vigorous, and quite disappointing. Some years ago, gardeners in the Deep South used to get plants budded on Texas Wax— but this seems to have vanished entirely. Some believe that the great rose fields in Texas depend on these roots, but most of them are budded on multiflora.

Some local rose nurserymen in this area still bud on *R. odorata*, as do a few in California; the resulting plants are fine, even when the water table tends to be high. (Dr. Huey will produce good plants in Florida and along the hotter reaches of the Gulf Coast, but it will not do its best near a high water table.)

Possibly the double, white Cherokee rose, *R. fortuneana*, is the best of all rootstocks for this region—if you can still find it.

GOING BY THE GRADE

The top grade in roses is "#1, two year, field grown." This contains the cream of the crop and should always be your first choice. Plants in this grade will have at least three canes, 18 inches or more long, before pruning prior to shipping.

Where the budget is strained to cover the required number of plants, there are two alternatives. First, see if in your selection most of your varieties are the newer, patented varieties. If so, it is possible to substitute some of the really fine, but older, kinds whose patents have expired; many of these are the backbone of fine rose gardens everywhere. The savings here can be substantial.

Smaller savings can be made by dropping down to the grade "#1½, two year, field grown." This will have at least two canes, 15 inches long, before pruning. These are good, sound plants, but it may take them a year of growing on to become a number-one grade.

The number-two grade need have as few as one cane, 12 inches long—so it is seldom worth planting.

BARE ROOT OR POTTED?

Bare-root, dormant plants are best; they should always be used where possible. When planting is delayed until late in the spring, however, potted roses—in full growth—can be planted. But while these are useful for replacing a dead plant during the growing season, they have two disadvantages. First, when they are potted their roots have to be cut severely to fit into the container, which greatly weakens the plants. Second, when they are planted the roots they do have are already formed in a tight circle, a pattern they seldom break out of in later life. With the restricted root run, the plant has a very limited access to nutrients and water, woefully restricting its growth.

There is one way out. Just before growth starts in the following spring, lift the plant carefully and, just as carefully, unwind the roots. (A chopstick, or similar piece of smooth wood, will be useful in this.) A stream of water from a hose may be necessary to get the core of soil loose without tearing the roots badly. Then replant the bush, spreading the roots over a cone of back-fill soil in the usual way.

The packaged "preplanted" roses found in some supermarkets and variety stores demand that the plants (both tops and roots) be so severely pruned to fit the too-small containers that they are not worth notice. Even if they were given away, in most brands, they would be too expensive—in terms of your time, space, labor, and materials—and would produce little to show for your efforts.

WHEN THE PLANTS ARRIVE

Most roses are now packed in plastic bags or sheets, and they travel much better than they used to. Still, just as soon as a shipment is received it should be checked. Make certain that the proper number of plants of the right varieties are included. Then check the condition of the plants.

If the roots are dry, plunge them into a bucket of lukewarm water for a couple of hours. Check the bark on the canes. If it is dull and shriveled, the roses can be restored to full vigor by the following techniques. If they are to go into the ground in a day or two, soak the whole plant in lukewarm water, preferably overnight. If planting is to be delayed for a longer period, dig a trench in a shaded spot and bury the plants, making certain that there is good contact of the soil with the canes. If the soil is dry, water well after covering.

If the plants are in good condition and planting is to be delayed for a few days, water the roots a bit, replace the wrappings, and store in a cool, dark place. For a delay of more than four or five days, dig a trench in a shady spot and heel in the plants, covering only the roots with soil. Wrapping the tops in damp burlap will help if the weather isn't too cold. Water the cover every day or so. If the buds should start to grow, remove the burlap. If a shady spot is not available, cover the canes as well.

PREPARING THE SITE

Those fortunate souls with a good, well-drained deep loam to work with do not have to prepare whole beds for their roses. All they have to do is peel off the existing turf and spade deeply as they prepare the individual holes. When they plant they use the usual back-fill mixture of equal parts good soil, peat moss or compost, and sharp sand. In areas where sharp sand is not available, such as at least parts of the Southeast, horticultural-grade perlite can be used. The stark white color is not attractive, but when the mulch is applied this is hidden.

Those of us who have less favorable conditions can do a better job of upgrading the planting site by working over the whole bed at one time.

Where the soil is reasonably good, bed making is quite simple. Remove the turf and pile it "wrong side up." Then remove the topsoil and pile it. Remove enough subsoil to make the bed 14 to 16 inches deep. Scatter a generous amount of agricultural lime on the bottom of the bed if the pH is less than 6.0 or if the subsoil is on the heavy side. Two to three pounds will be enough for each hundred square feet in light soils. On good loams increase this to five or six pounds; on heavy soils 10 to 12 pounds are required. These amounts will raise the pH one full point. Use gypsum (land plaster) if the pH is above 6.0. Then add triple superphosphate. Cover the bottom with the turfs, still top side down, and dig over the whole area thoroughly, a full spade depth deep. If the bed is large, a rotary tiller can reduce the work load greatly. To get the tiller into the bed, leave a ramp of soil at one end. When the work is finished only this ramp will have to be done by hand.

Put back the topsoil, enriched with peat moss or compost and sharp, granular sand, usually in equal portions. If necessary, use subsoil with the same additions to top off the bed, which should be an inch or two above the surrounding soil, to allow for settling. The bed should be ready for planting in four to six weeks.

Where the soil is really poor, either very sandy or heavy clay, heroic measures are needed. After saving the turfs and whatever topsoil there is, remove the subsoil to a depth of 18 to 20 inches. Break up the bottom a full spade depth after adding lime and superphosphate and the turfs. Where the soil is on the light side, add good topsoil, and either compost or peat moss to the soil removed, and fill the bed. Where the soil is very heavy, double the proportions of sand and humus (using liberal amounts of manure when available). In the mixing, add liberal amounts of either agricultural lime or gypsum, whichever is needed to bring the pH to between 5.5 and 6.5.

SCHEDULING THE HARD WORK

Making a bed this way is a lot of hard work—there is no question about it. When a first-rate job is done, however, the bed will grow fine roses for years. When short-cuts are resorted to, the roses will not do as well and the whole job will have to be redone in a few years. In other words, the man-hours *per year* are really less for the very best preparation, and the number and quality of blooms will be far greater.

It should be noted, too, that all of this work does not have to be done at once. Just schedule your time so that the bed will be finished four to six weeks before the plants will be available for planting. In other words, do just as much at a time as is comfortable. The only alternative is to divide the planting between two or more planting seasons.

BED LEVELS

There is no one answer to the question of what is the proper bed level, after settling of the soil. In most areas, a bed level equal to the surrounding area or an inch below is about right. In arid areas a level three or four inches lower is a big help in irrigation. In areas where the water table is close to the surface, as in Norfolk, much of Florida, and the Gulf Coast, the level should be from four to six inches higher, retaining that level with a high curb.

WHEN TO PLANT

In areas of severe climate, spring planting is best. The proper time is just as soon as the soil is workable. The test for this is simple. Press a small amount of soil into a ball. If it holds its shape when tapped rather briskly, it is too wet to work; when it crumbles, it is ready. Fall planting is better in other areas, as the plant, without great stress to the portions above ground, has time to establish a good root system before having the added burden of top growth. A minimum of four weeks, and better six, before expected freeze-up should be allowed. In the mildest areas, such as Florida, November is the usual time for planting.

THE ACTUAL PLANTING

When the bushes are in good shape for planting, the holes must be dug before the plants are taken to the garden. In beds it is wise to use a line to true up the holes.

Each hole should be 18 inches wide and 12 inches deep. If the roots are too large to fit, don't cramp them—make the hole larger. In very good soil, if single holes are used, sprinkle some superphosphate and agricultural limestone in the bottom and work it in several inches deep, then make a cone-shaped mound of the back-fill mixture in the center of the hole. You are ready to plant.

Not until now should the first plants be taken from their storage place, and not more than eight or ten should be taken at a time. Place them in a bucket half filled with water and cover them with damp burlap. Be certain that you have the proper plants to fit your plan. Don't forget that just a few moments of sun and wind can kill the tender feeding root hairs, which are essential to quick establishment of the plant, so never take more than one plant at a time from the bucket and keep the others covered.

Prune any broken canes or roots, then place the plant over a cone of soil, spreading the roots thoroughly. If the roots won't fit, don't curl them around the hole or cut them off—make the hole larger. Back-fill with the prepared soil, packing the soil firmly around the roots so there are no air pockets.

PROPER DEPTH

The depth of the bud union (a swelling of the stem just above the roots) in planting depends to a considerable extent on the climate. This union shows as a bulge between the roots and the canes. In severe climates this should be about two inches below the surface. In mild climates it should be at the surface, and where the plants hardly go dormant in the winter, it should be an inch or so above. All of these measurements should be made *after* the plant has been firmed into the soil. If an adjustment has to be made, don't pull the plant to make adjustments; dig it up. This saves the fine root hairs from being torn.

FINISHING THE PLANTING

When the proper depth has been established, fill the hole about three-quarters full. Slowly pour on a bucket of water. Do this to a number of plants at a time. When the water has seeped in for ten minutes or so, fill the holes, lightly—don't press down. When soil is that wet, pressure will destroy its structure by closing the pores, and that results in poor root growth. Build a mound of soil in the center of the plant six to eight inches high. After good growth has started, progressively pull down this cone until the bed is level.

Some growers add a spoonful of soluble fertilizer to the water used in settling the plant. No other fertilizer should be used at this time. When the plants have become established, in about six weeks, they should be given a feeding of complete fertilizer. Then the summer mulch should be put on.

Chapter 4

High Pruning and Its Variations

It is probable that more gardeners are confused about pruning than any other phase of rose growing. The pity is that there is little if any reason for this confusion.

It can be granted that rose growing was almost ruined by the excessive pruning of a half a century and more ago. But reason, based on a better knowledge of plant growth, has changed all that. It is now understood that you just can't remove three quarters or more of the top of a *hardy shrub* and expect to have a healthy and *long-lived* plant. All the lost stored food in the wood, and the lost food-producing capacity in the reduced foliage, precludes that.

Essentially, pruning comes down to this. What do you want from the plant? Anything that stands in the way of this ideal should be removed. It's that simple!

YOUR GOAL

Different people grow roses for different reasons. Most grow them for their color and beauty in the garden, with a few of the blooms cut for arrangements in the home. Such folk prune moderately, assuring themselves of a large number of really nice blooms on moderately long stems. Those few who demand near perfection, either for exhibition or for very special arrangements, will prune more severely and will disbud, so that only a single bloom will be produced on each long stem. Large size and perfect shape can only be attained by sacrificing a considerable quantity of bloom. The lightest pruning of all is reserved for the Polyanthas, Floribundas, Species and Old roses. Here only dead, pest-ridden, or out-of-scale wood is ever touched. (Climbers, Tree roses, and espalier roses are discussed in sections that follow.)

BASIC PRUNING

Much of the complexity of pruning vanishes when the operation is taken a step at at time. The first step is to cut out all dead and diseased wood. Where only part of a cane is removed, make the cut just above a bud. If a stub is left it will die back and offer an entrance to rot or borers. Where the whole cane is taken, make the cut flush with the supporting wood. Large cuts can be smoothed with a sharp knife.

For many years garden writers have stressed the necessity of painting pruning cuts more than half an inch in diameter with a "cane sealer" or tree-wound paint. They claim that if this is not done either rots will devastate the tissue or borers will invade it. But unless cane borers are a constant problem in the area, forget the whole thing. On the other hand, where it is found that prevention is necessary, tree-wound paint, shellac, or proprietary sealers can be used. Letting the wound dry for three to five days before sealing will increase the time the sealer will remain effective.

SPRING PRUNING

As soon as the winter protection is removed, the mulch should be pulled back, exposing all of the above-ground growth. All of this growth should be examined carefully for canker. Shriveled spots or entirely encircled canes are all too common. Infected wood should be cut back to clean tissue, and the trimmings should be *burned*—not just thrown away. Many growers spray the canes and soil with a "dormant strength" lime-sulfur spray, just before growth starts. No controlled research has ever been published on this, and some growers question its value. On the other hand, no one has ever proved that it didn't help control canker. Take your choice; *I* don't—and have almost no canker.

REMOVING THE TWIGGY GROWTH

The slender twiggy growth common to all roses, and more especially to Polyanthas and Floribundas, will never produce flowers. Remove all of it, cutting flush at the base.

With all dead, diseased, and nonproductive wood removed, the next step is to open the center of the plant so that air and light can penetrate readily. This speeds drying of the foliage, which in turn reduces the spread of diseases. Also, if the plant is allowed to become too dense, some inner leaves will become too shaded when full growth is reached; they will then yellow and fall.

THE FINAL CUTS

All the remaining spring pruning depends on just two factors—the final size of the plant and its shape. The size depends on the inherent vigor of the cultivar, the climate and the soil involved, and the quality of the culture. The difference in size between two cultivars in a given group can be quite startling, especially when grown side by side. Compare the two Floribundas, Gold Cup and Frensham. Gold Cup grew for me (at Biltmore House, North Carolina) with quite slender canes to about 16 inches. In the same garden Frensham regularly grew well above four feet in height, with heavy canes. Such differences should be considered in the planning stage, as pruning alone cannot keep them equal in size.

The differences in the size of plants of the same cultivar under different conditions of soil and climate can be equally great. Years ago I used to top my Betty Priors at six feet (in Massachusetts) because my very short mother couldn't cut blooms higher than that. Some years after that, as editor of publications for the American Rose Society, I compiled the reports for the "Proof of the Pudding" section of the *American Rose Annual*. The average height of Betty Prior, nationwide, was about 39 inches! Some of the plants in that average must have been pretty small.

All of these differences must be considered when you make the final decision on the severity of the final cuts. Start with a middle-of-the-road approach—that is, by taking a quarter to a third off the top. Modifications—up or down—can be made in future years to fit your own garden requirements.

The final touches are added when "shaping cuts" remove the excessive height of extra-vigorous shoots to fit them into the overall shape of the plant.

REMOVING SUCKERS

From time to time most roses send up vigorous shoots from the rootstock; they are called "suckers." Blooms from multiflora rootstock are small and white (much like

Regardless of the design style, roses can add color
and a softening grace. Here the severe modern treatment
is saved from an almost harsh plainness
by just a few well-grown roses.

blackberry flowers); their odor is not pleasant. The blooms from Dr. Huey rootstock are nicer, being single and dark red, with golden stamens, but they are not the variety you bought. Any cane that grows from below the bud union should be removed with a flush cut. Identification of suckers is quite simple, as the leaves of multiflora are rather small and a somewhat dull, light green. The leaves of Dr. Huey are dark and have a distinctive reddish cast.

SUMMER PRUNING

In the bad old days of hard pruning it was considered necessary to remove half of the top of all plants at the end of the first flush of bloom. In addition, all feeding and most watering was suspended for the summer. The rationale was that the plants needed time to rest and gain strength for the fall bloom. July and August, in those days, were pretty bleak in the rose garden! Such a program was, of course, just the reverse of what the plants needed. Every ounce of cane and every leaf cut reduced the food and the food-producing capacity of the plant. Also, with fertilizers withheld and water reduced, the plants hardened and made little new growth. The fall bloom was reduced, rather than enhanced.

Now, with pruning only for shape, plus good fertilization and water management, growth never slows and fall bloom is glorious.

Most of the shaping pruning should be done when blooms are cut. Whether blooms are cut for the home or faded blooms are cut to prevent seed formation—reducing later bloom—the cuts should not be deep. Normally, the cuts should be made just above the first or, at most, the second five-leaflet leaf. Excessively vigorous "blind shoots" (they produce only leaves with no blooms) must be cut to their base.

DISBUDDING

When especially large and lovely blooms are desired, either for exhibition at a flower show or for some very special arrangement, Hybrid Teas, Hybrid Perpetuals, and Grandifloras should have all but the terminal bud removed. The side buds should be twisted out early or a noticeable scar will remain—which in flower-show competition will result in a loss of points. Those gardeners who enjoy the mass display in the garden never disbud, as it greatly reduces the total number of blooms.

FALL PRUNING

In severe climates, fall pruning is self-defeating. If you cut the plant to the size you want in the spring, winterkill will, almost without exception, cut further into the plant. It is better to wait until spring, see how much damage you have, and then prune. There is one major exception to this: overly long shoots should be cut back to the main body of the plant just as soon as the leaves have fallen. If they are left until spring, winter winds can whipsaw them and rock the plant to the point where considerable root damage will be done.

This blanket stricture on fall pruning in severe climates must, of course, be cut to fit the pattern of winter protection used. Those who use the new plastic shelters, naturally, have to prune the canes to fit. But the major principle holds—don't cut more than you have to.

In relatively mild climates cut only over-long shoots.

In semitropical areas, where roses are *evergreen shrubs*, the situation is quite different. The old, established custom was to prune hard after the summer rains— in September or October. This will either kill the bush or stunt it for the rest of its shortened life. The modern approach makes the rose truly perennial in this area. When the plant is as nearly dormant as it will ever get (January–February), get rid of the dead, diseased, and twiggy growth. Most growers say that the remaining growth should be cut to 18 inches, but don't rely on inches as a measure. Cut *up to* 50 percent of the tops. In this way each cultivar will reach its own potential, which means that, under good cultural conditions, two or three times the usual spacing must be given, as huge plants result from all varieties—up to five feet across and eight feet tall!

GROUP DIFFERENCES

These general principles must be tailored somewhat for some classes of roses. They are designed especially for Hybrid Teas, Grandifloras, Hybrid Perpetuals, and the strong-growing Floribundas. Light-caned Floribundas, on the other hand, need only the removal of dead, diseased, and twiggy growth. Proper cutting of faded blooms will take care of the rest.

Shrub roses, especially cultivars such as Golden Wings, develop differently from most of the common cultivars. It takes two or three years to build a sound framework for the plant. During this period no pruning at all should be given, and after that only light shaping is necessary. Species roses generally fall into the same pattern. After these plants get older, however, it becomes necessary to remove some of the older canes periodically, to make room for new canes to develop.

The Old roses vary tremendously, but, generally speaking, they need little pruning beyond the pattern for the Shrub roses. Here, however, as with the Shrubs that bloom but once, the faded blooms should be allowed to produce their seed capsules (hips), which are often very decorative. Some few, like the Rugosas, are recurrent in their bloom, and have hips as attractive as the blooms themselves, so these should be left alone.

CLIMBERS

Climbing Hybrid Teas and Floribundas bloom on wood produced in the current season, so they are handled just like their bushy counterparts. Large-Flowered Climbers and Ramblers, however, bloom on laterals from old wood. Those which bloom but once should be pruned just after the blooms fade. The oldest canes should be cut to their bases. Then cut lateral canes to six to ten inches. If more new canes grow than were removed, select only the best by midsummer and cut out those remaining. Tie the selected canes into position at this time. Some of the faded blooms can be left on the plant if the attractive hips are desired in the fall.

With cultivars that have recurring bloom, however, faded blooms should be removed regularly—otherwise the repeat bloom will be reduced. Other pruning for this group should be limited to the removal of growth beyond the allotted space, as the older wood produces the most bloom.

MINIATURES AND TREES

Miniature roses tend to revert every once in a while and send up strong canes. These should be cut off at the base. Little other pruning is necessary, unless there is an excess of twiggy growth or some dieback.

Tree roses must be rather severely pruned or the head will become too heavy for the stem to hold. Canes are usually reduced to six to ten inches and their number held constant—for every new cane allowed to grow, an old one must be removed.

Chapter 5

Fertilizers – Up to Date

Proper feeding of roses does not require much time or labor, but it does require considerable study and observation. The whole problem is a bit complex, because no two soils are alike and differing climates also have an influence.

On the brighter side is the fact, once again, that roses are hardy shrubs—they will grow acceptably under a wide range of conditions. But if you are after the greatest number of large, well-colored blooms possible on vigorous plants, special attention to feeding is imperative.

SOIL TESTING—THE NEGLECTED KEY

There is one way to determine the major framework of a good feeding program: have your soil tested. This is a simple procedure, and it yields valuable information —yet all too many gardeners neglect it. They feed their plants by generalized instructions on the fertilizer bag. This is folly.

Soil samples can be tested at most county extension service offices or colleges of agriculture, either at no charge or for a small fee. For details get in touch with your local county agricultural agent. The reports generally give the levels of the major elements and the pH. Then recommendations are made as to what is needed. Be certain to mention on the sample that roses are to be the crop, as the recommendations will be different from those for a crop such as corn or alfalfa.

In areas where there are chronic shortages of certain elements, such as boron in parts of Florida, a more detailed analysis may be desired. This is available from commercial soil-testing laboratories, some of which even specialize in tests for rose growing. Such tests are also valuable where the soil conditions are far from ideal, as in the "sand hills" of the Carolinas or the very alkaline areas of the Southwest.

HOME TESTS

There are a number of do-it-yourself kits for testing soils. I would say that, while a professional job is called for at the outset, these home kits have a real value for continued monitoring of the fertility levels in the garden. With the advent of soluble fertilizers and frequent applications, a continued monitoring is worthwhile.

BEGINNING A FEEDING PROGRAM

When the results of the soil test are at hand, a feeding program can be put together. The first step is to bring the soil up to optimum conditions. Just as important are the following applications to keep the fertility level as nearly constant as possible.

The desired levels for the "major elements" are:

nitrogen: 25–50 parts per million

phosphorus: 5–10 parts per million

potash: 20–40 parts per million

calcium: 150 parts per million

WHAT THE ELEMENTS DO

All of the fertilizing elements necessary for robust plant growth—there are more than twenty of them—are not used in any one fertilizing program. Most "complete fertilizers" contain only the three major elements—nitrogen, phosphorus, and potash, always listed in that order—plus some other elements—not listed on the label—as impurities, notably sulfur. Calcium is the only other element that is used regularly, and then only every three years or so.

All of the minor elements are assumed to be in the soil in sufficient quantities. Most soil tests do not check for these, but if our assumption is wrong the plants will tell us by clear symptoms of poor growth.

Where the amounts of the major elements used each year may be great, the amounts of the others are very small, even as little as one or two parts per million, as with boron; 15 parts per million of this element can be *toxic!*

There are certain areas of the country, however, that do have a general lack of one or more of these. This is generally well known in the areas involved, and local fertilizer plants add traces of the needed elements in their products. To a great extent this eliminates the problem.

NITROGEN

This is the prime element for growth. Where too little is present, growth is restricted. Where there is too much, growth is rapid and the stems and leaves are soft and weak. Nitrogen moves more rapidly through the soil than the other elements, so it can be lost through subsurface drainage during excessively wet periods. Because of this it is wise to give repeated applications, and to provide part of the requirements in a slow-release form, which will not leach. Nitrogen is also the most expensive of the major elements.

Deficiency symptoms: There is little growth, and the leaves are yellowish, sometimes with red or purple veins. Blooms are sparse, small, and off color.

PHOSPHORUS

The growth that nitrogen produces in canes, leaves, and roots is made sturdy by phosphorus. Leaves will be large and blooms will have good color. This element makes less movement through the soil than any other—it gets tied up with other elements very easily, all too often in forms unavailable to plants. Putting super-phosphate on the surface of the soil is an exercise in futility; practically none will reach the root zone. For best results, incorporate it in the bottom of the beds or planting holes before the bush is planted. For later applications, dig it in—even if some roots are damaged in the process. Fall applications of superphosphate are much more effective than those given in late winter or early spring—unless it is applied as a foliar spray. Where the pH is low, the availability of phosphorus is greatly reduced.

Deficiency symptoms: Leaves are small and have purple edges and even spots on the blades. Stems are thin and woody.

POTASSIUM

The effects of potassium on growth are hard to pinpoint, but it is absolutely necessary. Like phosphorus, this element hardens the canes, leaves, and roots, mainly by increasing the production of sugars and starches, thus making the plants more vigorous and hardy. Clay soils are apt to be high in potassium and they do not tie it up in forms which the plants can't use, as they do with phosphorus. On the other hand, high-humus and very sandy soils lose potash readily; it moves through the soils fairly rapidly. With these soils particularly, give repeated, small applications, rather than one big one in the early spring. Where potassium is in ample supply, stress during periods of drought is lessened.

Deficiency symptoms: Old leaves turn dull, the margins show yellowing and finally turn brown—and die. Plants are stunted.

CALCIUM

The need for calcium is varied. It shows up in the composition of plant tissues, but its effects on the soil and soil organisms are of greater importance. It aids in opening the tight structure of clay soils, and when humus is added, aids in the formation of "crumb structure" in sandy soils as well. Beyond this, calcium encourages the activities of the microorganisms present, which enhance the availability of many other elements. As agricultural limestone, the usual source of calcium, takes a long time to break down and become available, it is usually applied only every three years; annual applications will certainly cause trouble. This material is highly alkaline, so avoid its use where the soil or the irrigation water is also. Gypsum "land plaster" is a good neutral source—and it is more rapid acting, too.

Deficiency symptoms: New growth dies back, growth stiffens, and leaves are mottled, finally showing dead spots in the center.

MAGNESIUM

The real importance of magnesium is often overlooked. It is necessary for the formation of chlorophyll, without which plants will die. Where dolomitic limestone is used as a source of calcium, magnesium levels should be adequate, as both elements are in it. But if the calcium levels are very high, the magnesium will be made unavailable to the plants. For a quick cure, spray the plants, leaves and all, with Epsom salts, one tablespoon per quart of water to the point of runoff. For a more lasting treatment, dust the soil *only*—not the plant—lightly with finishing lime from your hardware or building supply dealer. One application should last two to three years.

Deficiency symptoms: Leaves turn reddish or purple between the veins and dead spots appear. Leaves drop early.

SULFUR

Most soils have ample sulfur, since it is present in many fertilizers, as ammonium sulfate, for example. Without sulfur the formation of proteins comes to a halt; so, too, does the formation of plant hormones—which regulate growth.

Deficiency symptoms: Older leaves show a yellowish cast, and this progresses up to the newer leaves.

IRON

Most soils, especially reddish ones, have plenty of iron, but if the pH gets too high it can become unavailable. It is necessary for the production of chlorophyll. Lowering the pH will take care of many troubles, but using chelated iron—under any of a number of trade names—will give longer lasting results.

Deficiency symptoms: Intervein portions of leaves get progressively lighter; in extreme cases even the veins bleach and the whole leaf becomes cream colored. These symptoms start at the top of the plant and work down.

Roses don't have to be grown in special gardens;
they can be used in many parts of the landscape.
Here they define the curve of the driveway
and accent the ground-cover junipers.

*Low-growing Polyanthas and Floribundas
can add a cheery note
to any entrance.*

TRACE ELEMENTS

Such elements as copper, boron, zinc, or manganese seldom give trouble in good garden soils. Muck or high-humus soils do sometimes lack copper. Four ounces of copper sulfate per thousand square feet should clear that up.

Some fairly well defined areas in the country do have problems regularly. Parts of Florida lack boron, zinc, and copper, for example. Parts of California are shy of boron and zinc. In these areas it is wise to buy locally formulated fertilizers, which have the necessary trace elements for these special conditions.

SOURCES OF FERTILITY

Just how to apply the needed materials, and when, is the major problem. Today we have materials old and new with which to feed our plants. In spite of what the organic gardeners claim, several different sources of fertility should be used if the best results are to be obtained. The sources are many. The older kinds include manures, other organic matter, and "commercial" fertilizers of many formulations. The newer "slow release" fertilizers are invaluable in maintaining even growth over a long period. New liquid "foliar" types are unequaled for speed in correcting deficiencies as well as keeping plants growing steadily. Trace elements in the newer "fritted" or "chelated" forms release their nutrients more evenly than older sources.

By choosing wisely among these, one can produce good growth of roses *all season long* and bring the bushes into winter well hardened and vigorous. They will thus be able to withstand the rigors of winter and start off the spring with strong growth.

ANIMAL MANURES

From the beginning of agriculture and gardening until little more than a century ago, animal manures were the mainstay of any fertilization program—some other organic materials, such as fish or meat scraps, seaweeds, and bones, were used as well—but these materials are becoming increasingly scarce and expensive in most parts of the country. They are best used when mixed with some sort of "bedding," whether this be straw, coarse peat moss, bagasse (sugar cane residue), or even leaves. All kinds should be aged to some degree, with poultry manures needing a couple of months. Horse manure is "hot"—that is, it builds heat during initial decomposition—so it must be composted until this heat is gone.

The actual amount of fertility in manures is low, and the elements are rarely balanced. The main benefits come from the organic matter, some trace elements, "soil flora" (bacteria and fungi), and possibly some hormones.

FERTILITY VALUES OF ANIMAL MANURES

	%N	%P	%K	Comments
Horse	0.76	0.56	0.65	Best for clay, good for all soils
Cow	0.4	0.3	0.44	Best on loams and light soils
Pig	0.3	0.3–0.4	0.45	Must be composted
Poultry	1.8	1.0	0.5	Must be composted. 1–2% calcium
Rabbit	2.0–5.0	1.0–3.3	2.0–5.0	Varies widely with diet

Fertility Values of Animal Manures *(Continued)*

	%N	%P	%K
Sheep & goats	0.65	0.46	0.23
Spent mush- room manure*	1.0	1.0	1.0

*Still retains some fertility and organic material.

Commercial Manures

In most areas cow, steer, sheep, and poultry manures are available dried and shredded. These products are clean, odorless, and generally have more of the major elements. On the other hand, many of the beneficial effects of the soil microorganisms, hormones, and vitamins are lost.

N–P–K Content of Dried Manures*

	%N	%P	%K	Comment
Cattle	1.3	0.9	0.8	Steer manure is higher in all three, especially when it comes from feedlots
Sheep & goats	2.5	1.5	1.5–3.0	
Poultry	4.5	3.2	1.3	

* These figures for nitrogen, phosphorus, and potash apply to natural manures only. Some brands have added mineral nutrients; check the label. (Dog manure should never be used, as it contains acids that harm plants.)

Other Organic Sources

Other sources of organic fertilizers are legion, but most of them are available only in restricted areas. Sphagnum peat moss and compost, however, are almost universally available; the latter being homemade. But here again it is the humus content of most of these materials that is the most important, for if they are purchased for their fertility alone they are generally wildly expensive.

An exception of some importance can be made for muck soil to beef up the very sandy soils in some parts of the deepest South, especially Florida. Granted, this material breaks down quite rapidly—all humus does under hot-moist conditions lasting much of the year—but the results seem worthwhile if it is renewed—and renewed and renewed—over the years.

Another, wider exception should always be kept in mind. If you live near an abandoned sawmill, use sawdust. If you are nearer a distillery, use spent brewers grains. If on a coast, use seaweed, kelp preferred. In other words, use what is close at hand and *reasonable in price!*

Chemical Fertilizers

Today it is fashionable to decry chemical fertilizers—especially among organic gardeners. This is rubbish! Both chemical and organic sources should be used for best results. After all, they must be broken down into the needed elements before the plants will benefit from either—and these elements are identical regardless of their source!

The chemicals have some important characteristics. It is possible to proportion the mixture to exactly what is needed in the soil for any specific crop. Many of the compounds are rather fast acting, but some are much slower. These materials are uniform—not a strong point with many of the organics—which makes it simple to apply just the right amount every time. Too, most are universally available, and per-unit cost of the desired elements—not counting fillers at any value—is very low. But perhaps more important, any elements desired can be combined in exactly the amounts needed to fit the demands of *your* soil. Acid, neutral, and alkaline formulations can be mixed in almost endless numbers—and further, although a large number of formulations are readily available, home mixing can tailor the product to special needs.

It is also a simple matter to use a single element or even a pair, a need that occurs often during the growing season, when a do-it-yourself soil test indicates that the balance desired has not been reached. While there are any number of sources for single elements, here are some of the best:

Nitrogen
Ammonium sulfate: 20% N (acid, gets my vote)
Ammonium nitrate: 30% N (acid, careful! it can burn)
Sodium nitrate: 16% N (alkaline)
Urea: 40% N (very rapid action, use carefully)
Phosphorus
Triple superphosphate: 45% P (neutral, very slow)
Potash
Potassium sulfate: 50% K (acid, easy to use, fine)
Kainite: 15% K (generally used only in soils deficient in magnesium, which it contains)
But regular fertilizers have drawbacks, too. They are usually very fine grained and dusty. They can't be applied when the foliage is wet or when it is windy; any

that falls on the leaves will burn. Some manufacturers "pelletize" the mixture. This makes application easy, clean, and much safer.

SLOW-RELEASE TYPES

Urea and formaldehyde are combined under varying temperatures and pressures to make a wide range of different materials, varying from indestructible buttons to a high-grade (38% N) nitrogen fertilizer. The beauty of this material (Uramite) is that, when in the soil with water, soil microorganisms, and warmth, it breaks down slowly and quite evenly over a long period. However, it requires a matter of weeks before the first nitrogen is available to plants; the time varies with the seasons. In some formulations only part of the required nitrogen is supplied in this way.

When a slow-release, "complete" fertilizer is desired, the new *coated* fertilizers are used. One, called Osmocote, comes in several formulations, and you have your choice of applications that last three to four months or eight to nine months!

FOLIAR FERTILIZERS

Possibly even more important than the slow release types are the new so-called foliar fertilizers. These are liquids that can be applied directly to the leaves and canes, or to the soil, or both. They come in a good number of different formulations to fit differing needs, and are the most rapidly acting fertilizers known.

The labor of applying them is almost nil. They can be added to the irrigation water or, more generally, added to the spray mix. Applications are usually made every two to three weeks, but by varying the proportions this can be adjusted downward. To lengthen the intervals really defeats the main purpose—to keep the plants growing constantly and evenly.

Another advantage of the foliars is that they can be used later in the season than the mineral types, without danger of late, soft growth liable to winter damage. In fact, the effect is exactly the opposite. The elements are taken into the plants within hours, and by increasing the food supply in the sap, make the plant hardier.

THE MASTER PLAN

THE FIRST YEAR

If the beds have been properly made and aged, no fertilizer is needed at planting time, except for the possible addition of a little soluble fertilizer to the water used to settle the soil. Just as soon as the leaves have developed, however, start feeding them with a foliar feed. And instead of feeding every three weeks, feeding every 10 to 12 days *at reduced strength* will give the plants a constant and even nutrient level. Some growers like to shift to a high phosphorus formulation, such as Peters 15–30–15, when buds first appear, and continue until the leaves drop in the fall. In any event, it is wise to resort to a lower nitrogen formula than Ra-Pid-Gro 23–21–19 after September.

After the newly set plants have made six weeks of growth in the spring, apply one quarter of a year's requirement of a balanced mineral fertilizer in a ratio that matches the recommendations of the soil test report. If no such ratio is available, you can mix your own from the materials listed on page 59. It is best if half the nitrogen comes from mineral sources, for quick action, and the other half from either organic or slow-release sources. Six weeks later, duplicate this application. (In areas where the growing season is long, the amounts can be reduced proportionately and three applications can be made.) In severe climates no mineral fertilizers should be given after the first of July, in milder areas not later than August 15.

It doesn't take much room to create a beauty spot.
By adding a Climber on the fence,
the beauty is doubled.

In areas of severe winters a "hardening feeding" should be given. Here no nitrogen is given, only phosphorus and potash to harden growth already made. At your farm supply store they will have "small grain formulations," such as 0–12–12 or 0–14–14. Apply this six to eight weeks before the expected time of freeze-up. If the season is dry, water well the day before and then water the formulation in thoroughly.

Succeeding Years

The only change in subsequent years is to apply the remaining half of the year's requirements. This may be done in late winter or just after pruning and cleanup are finished, and before the new mulch is put on.

Chapter 6

Mulches

MULCHES AND THE NEGLECT OF THE HOE

It used to be that when the weather got hot the gardener got hotter—hoeing the rose beds. The first consideration, of course, was getting rid of weeds. But the making of a dust mulch was a close second, for that would conserve moisture. The weeds were eliminated, but at times the roots of the roses were damaged. Worse still, a slip of the hoe would damage the stems of the plant, offering an entrance to canker. As for the dust mulch, it did conserve moisture but was destroyed with every rain and had to be rebuilt.

Today the hoe is used only on the spring cleanup. After that the bed is fertilized and a mulch laid down.

WHAT IS A MULCH?

A mulch is any layer of material—organic or inorganic, although the organics are preferred—laid on the surface of the soil. The thickness of the material varies from a few thousandths of an inch for plastic sheets to two inches for peat moss, three to four inches for pine needles, or even six inches for spent hops (which settle greatly). A great many gardeners use mulches to keep down weeds and conserve moisture. Any good mulch will do both, but it will also provide a great many other benefits as well.

Important in some gardens is the reduction of erosion. Organic mulches, on disintegrating, add humus to the soil. The amount of fertilizing elements added from this breakdown is generally overestimated, but in some cases the tiny amounts of microelements are significant.

Under a mulch the soil structure tends to improve, and this in turn increases the interchange of air and soil atmosphere. Where there is an optimum amount of oxygen in the soil atmosphere, root growth is at its best, producing the most vigorous plants. In such a soil, too, soil microorganisms thrive, which helps with general nutrition. And under most mulches (not including black plastic) the soil temperatures are kept from wide fluctuations: in the summer the temperature is kept near optimum for root growth, and in the winter alternate freezing and thawing is reduced, preventing much root damage.

Finally, where the mulch is kept clean it acts as a physical barrier to disease, such as black spot.

There are other considerations, but these should show that mulches are just about indispensable.

MULCH MATERIALS — GOOD AND BAD

As with organic fertilizers, mulch materials must be chosen, to a great extent, not only for their desirability, but also on the basis of their availability and cost.

PINE NEEDLES (PINE STRAW IN THE SOUTH)

The long needles of the loblolly and long-leaf pines are preferred to the thin, shorter needles of the white and Virginia pines, but all are good. In many areas they are available in bales at a moderate cost.

These materials are long lasting and attractive in color, and the loose structure of the layer allows free exchange of air and water. Although they tend to blow and release little fertility when they finally decompose, they are among the best.

PEAT MOSS

Except for one fault, peat moss would be *the* ideal mulch. When it gets dry it forms a crust; this not only sheds later rains but impairs gaseous exchange. One way to get around this fault is to mix it with some coarse material; otherwise, light raking of the surface will correct it. Attractive in color, long lasting, and universally available at a reasonable cost, this mulch must be considered. While most gardeners use the horticultural grade, which lasts well, some prefer the poultry-litter grade, which is coarser. This reduces the crusting problem, lasts longer, and is usually cheaper. This material in a "used condition," complete with poultry manure, must be composted for at least three months before using, otherwise it will certainly burn. On decomposition, this material adds a little fertility and tends to be acid.

WOOD CHIPS (NUGGETS)

Raw wood chips have been around for a long time, on a local basis. Now they are being well processed in various grades, generally with added nutrients to aid in the decomposition without a nitrogen drain on the soil. The medium or coarse grades are best for mulching: these allow easy passage to both air and water; they have a pleasing, nonobtrusive color and last a long time.

Animal Manures

When mixed with good litter and aged somewhat (more than "somewhat" for horse manure), manures make a fine mulch from the growing standpoint, except for the almost inescapable weeds. Although the odor and the appearance are bad, the fertility, including trace elements, the soil flora, and the great humus value make these rate very high. If the cost is excessive, peat moss can be added.

Sawdust

Sawdust makes a good mulch if it is coarse and partly rotted. Fresh sawdust, two inches deep, should be treated with two pounds of ammonium sulfate per hundred square feet. (Wood shavings and excelsior make a poor mulch as they present a fire hazard, blow badly, and are unsightly. They can be composted, however.)

Leaves

The question is—which ones? Brittle leaves, such as oak or beech, are fine, especially if they have been put through a shredder set for a coarse grind. They have good color, don't mat in wet weather, have an acid reaction, and break down fairly slowly. Soft leaves, such as maple or birch, should never be used. When wet they form sodden barriers to both air and water; the roots beneath suffocate. Only thorough composting gives them any place in the garden.

HAY AND STRAW

Neither of these has any place in flower gardens, although in vegetable gardens and strawberry patches they do very well. They are miserably weedy, blow badly, and present a fire hazard, and the straw has an objectionable color. Legume hays are a different matter. Usually they are too expensive, but if you can find a bargain in old or moldy hay of soybeans, alfalfa, or clover you are lucky. A quick pass through the shredder helps here, too.

LAWN CLIPPINGS

No! They slow the flow of both air and water and often become very moldy and hot.

GROUND CORNCOBS

Where available, cobs are widely used. They mold badly in hot, wet weather, at first the color is too bright, and they don't last too long. They do provide fine growing conditions, and the cost is usually modest.

BAGASSE

A fine mulch, curiously neglected. It doesn't pack, lasts well, won't blow, and is almost fireproof. Many nurseries do not carry it but you can get it from farm stores as "poultry litter."

OTHER MATERIALS

Buckwheat hulls have good color and break down very slowly, but they blow badly and don't improve the soil much. Cottonseed hulls are good, where available. Spent hops make a fine, light mulch but settle greatly; two or three applications over several weeks are necessary to get a stable depth—but they are absolutely fireproof! Salt marsh hay and cranberry vines are very local. The hay will last for several years; both are generally used for winter mulches only.

MULCHES IN PRACTICE

When pruning, cleanup, and fertilization are finished in the spring, it is time to mulch. An exception is made for heavy clay soils; these should be allowed to warm considerably before putting on the mulch, even if this means another light hoeing.

Mulches should cover the whole root run, which in beds means the whole bed surface—except for a small circle around the canes of the plants. Most mulch materials are so moist during the growing season that actual contact with the basal canes can encourage diseases—canker, for example.

Many mulches settle to some degree, so it is wise to check from time to time and add more material as needed.

In the fall a mulch can keep a plant growing when it should be hardening its tissues against the coming cold. Then it is necessary to pull the mulch away; this dries the soil and helps the hardening process. By all means don't put on a winter mulch too early. Mice will move in and make their winter quarters there. When winter gets really rough they will depend on the bark and buds of your roses for food—quite effectively killing the plants.

EXTRA HELP—WEED KILLERS

Few mulches will control all weeds. Those which do grow, however, are usually easily pulled by hand. In very weedy soils, or where weed-infested materials are used (such as manure with straw litter), some help is needed. Weed killers that will do just that and not harm the roses are available—and more are coming along all the time. The granular formulation of Simazine is the only one I have used (on 6,000 roses at Biltmore Gardens), and it worked well. Check with your nurseryman for the kind that is preferred in your area.

It is wise to try a weed killer on a smaller corner of the garden before using it over-all. If the material is placed *on the soil surface* before the mulch is applied, use the amount recommended on the package. Don't go on the theory that "if a little is good, a lot will be better." You can kill plants that way!

On the other hand, if you apply the material on top of the mulch, the buffering effect of the mulch—different with each kind—will make stronger applications necessary for good control. You will have to apply progressively heavier amounts to your test section until you get the results you are after, without damage to the bushes. In the garden mentioned above we worked gradually to two and a half times normal amounts to overcome the buffering action of the two-inch-deep mulch of peat moss (horticultural grade). *Repeat applications* on the same mulch should be at or near *normal application rates*.

FOR WALKS

Walks of brick or gravel are hard to maintain, mainly because of weeds. A weed killer can be used here that will kill all kinds of plants—*but only if it will stay put after application*. Some kinds move laterally as well as vertically in the soil, and these would invade the beds and kill the roses. Amate-X is useful because it will not translocate. With care in applying it only to the walk, there is no danger to the near-by plants.

Chapter 7

Pest Control in Modern Terms

Great strides have been made in pest control in recent years—with the advent of both better materials and better equipment for applying them. By putting the best of both together, not only do the plants receive superior protection but the work load is reduced, sometimes dramatically.

SPRAY OR DUST?

There is no question about the relative worth of sprays and dusts in pest control. Sprays do a more thorough job, and they are cheaper, but that isn't the whole story. Spraying takes more time, for fresh solutions must be mixed for every application, and then the sprayer must be cleaned thoroughly and dried afterward. This isn't much where a large number of plants are involved, but where only a dozen or two plants are concerned, it can run to half the time spent.

With a duster, except for filling the hopper now and then, you start dusting at once, and when you are finished you just put the duster in the cabinet, ready for the next time. A distinct disadvantage of dusting is that you have to use the pesticide mixtures commercially available, as home mixing is hardly feasible. This can lead to the use of multipurpose mixtures when only one portion is needed—an added expense, as well as a violation of present-day concepts of "protecting the environment" against the unnecessary use of pesticides.

A way out for the gardener who has only a few plants, but who wants the flexibility and economy of spray control, is a hose-end sprayer. This doesn't produce as fine a spray as you would wish, or cover the underside of the leaves too easily, but with care good control is possible.

Up until a couple of years ago, these were the only options open. Now the engineers who developed the huge "mist blowers," used so effectively by orchardists and nurserymen, have come up with a scaled-down model suitable for use in home gardens. This opens marvelous possibilities.

Mist blowers inject the spray material into large volumes of air traveling at a very high rate of speed. The result is a mist, almost as fine as fog, that billows all over the plants—giving perfect coverage to all surfaces. As diseases are essentially eliminated, the plants grow better. Both time and effort are reduced dramatically, and the savings in materials required for superior coverage run as high as 80 percent. At the same time, spray burn is practically eliminated and unsightly spray residue is greatly reduced.

Anyone with a hundred or more plants should find such devices as the #1026 Airblast Atomist electric sprayer (Root-Lowell) a good investment and a great labor saver. The "cart-mounted" five-gallon model (#1027) is for gardens of 200 or more plants; it requires fewer fillings.

But what of those gardeners who have fewer plants? There are rumors that smaller models (powered by rechargeable batteries?) are on their way. If and when, they should be very popular.

If you do have only a few plants, dusting may be your choice for pest control. On the other hand, if you spray routinely, don't rule out *some* dusting. When you notice a few aphids or a bit of black spot during your five-minute prebreakfast stroll through the garden, it takes but a moment to give a quick shot of dust and prevent the trouble from spreading.

THE INSECT PESTS

It is easy to compile a list, as long as your arm, of insects that *can* attack roses. Such a list can scare you until you realize that very few *will actually show in any one location during any full growing season*. On top of that, most of those that do show up can be controlled with a single "broad spectrum" insecticide, such as Malathion or methoxychlor. Remember, too, that it is not necessary to use insecticides until the insects appear; however, with fungicides a regular schedule is necessary for prevention.

This takes care of most insects, but there are some that require special treatment.

THRIPS

Thrips are tiny, hair-thin animals that rasp their way into buds—out of the reach of sprays—and prevent the buds from opening. Don't confuse this effect with "balling," which is partly heredity and mostly the result of cool, wet weather. Where thrips are the cause, brownish streaks appear on the outer petals; with balling the outer petals are entirely brown. When the thrips start to fly, spray with Lindane every three to five days until the first bloom is well along. Later blooms seldom have much trouble. As thrips favor white or light colors, those who are especially plagued by them should choose their varieties accordingly.

"Red Spiders" or Mites

Technically the mites, of many kinds and colors, are not insects, but some of the broad spectrum insecticides (Malathion or Tedion) will control light infestations. But where the leaves take on a grayish cast and a light webbing is found under the leaves, stronger action must be taken. Kelthane, Aramite, or other acaracides should be sprayed several times to kill not only the adults but the eggs as well. Mites thrive in hot, dry weather.

Scales

It is true that scales can be controlled by spraying with Malathion, and so on, but that involves precise timing. They are only vulnerable when they emerge from under their scales and move to their new location. It is simpler to spray with a dormant-strength miscible oil *before growth starts in the spring.* A summer-strength oil spray (Volck) will control the crawlers, too.

Borers

The larvae of a number of insects tunnel in the canes or beneath the bark of roses. Those that gain entry through pruning cuts, such as the rose sawfly or the small carpenter bee, can be kept out by painting the cut surfaces with a tree-wound paint or shellac, or with a rose sealer from a small plastic applicator bottle. There are few

These are beautiful, well-grown plants,
with a good background. But they are too close
to the stepping stones—you would certainly
be scratched as you walked by.

areas where this is necessary. Those that gain entry through the side of the canes can only be controlled by cutting back to sound wood and burning the prunings.

DISEASES

BLACK SPOT AND MILDEW

Two diseases that still constitute the major problems for rose growers in most of the country, not including the Pacific Coast and some portions of the Southwest, are black spot and mildew. With the quite satisfactory modern fungicides, such as Manzate and Phaltan, black spot—the worst disease of the rose—could be controlled. To do this, however, requires careful spraying and a schedule that calls for an application every seven to ten days, oftener during wet weather, for the full growing season. During dry seasons the period could be increased—somewhat. That was the heaviest cultural load of the whole rose-growing program—it didn't even allow for a good vacation! When mildew showed up, it called for the addition of yet another fungicide, such as Mildex.

Recently a new material called Benlate has been stirring up all kinds of excitement—it looks like the biggest breakthrough in decades. It will *eradicate* mildew, even well-established mildew. Many rose growers have wiped out black spot entirely. The action of this new material is threefold: (1) it acts on contact, (2) it has a residual action on the leaf surface, and (3) it is a systemic—that is, it enters the plant and works from within. Systemics don't have to be renewed after every rain. As a result, the old weekly chore of spraying now becomes once in two weeks for most growers. A few claim they get good control by spraying only every three weeks. This means that the single greatest demand for labor in growing roses has been reduced by either 50 or 67 percent! And as an unexpected bonus, it has been found that Benlate controls mites as well.

Here and there we hear that some growers are not having these fabulous results, but it is too early to know why—the wide differences in climatic conditions no doubt affect the results considerably.

Those growers who want something providing more positive control could continue to add a reduced amount of Phaltan to the mix of Benlate.

At first, the price upset quite a few people—$25.00 for a two-pound package. But with fewer sprays necessary and one tablespoon making a full gallon of spray, they paid it. Now the price is down considerably, and may even go lower. If you put any value on your time and labor, it is a good investment. In addition, when a mist blower is involved, only about 25 percent of the "normal" amount of material is needed.

Finally, many knowledgeable growers claim that their healthier plants make better growth, produce more blooms and overwinter better than under any previous program. This is short of the ultimate goal of entirely disease-proof plants, or at least a "once-a-season" control method—but at this stage of the game, it is certainly a major breakthrough!

Rust

Mildew is almost universally found, and black spot is epidemic in most of the country. On the West Coast, however, and in parts of the Southwest, rust is the big problem. During wet periods—four hours or more of liquid water—and mild temperatures—60 to 75 degrees F.—the orange spots appear on the underside of the leaves. These mature as fluffy, reddish-orange masses of spores. Rust can entirely defoliate a bush in as little as five days, so watch for the first spots and spray with Phaltan or Captan at once. Dusting with sulfur works, too, but never use it when the temperature is 80 degrees F. or higher.

CANKER

The common (stem) canker is rightly named—most gardens have it to some degree. It enters the stems through wounds and produces almost black masses of spores just under the epidermis; if they surround the cane, it will die back to this point. Control consists of careful pruning—cutting out all dieback to sound wood—and keeping the hoe away from the canes. Brown canker has spots, often long and narrow, with purple edges, centers white at first, then light brown. Cut out badly infected canes in the spring and then spray thoroughly with dormant-strength lime-sulfur before growth starts.

GALLS

Crown gall is a most common disease, and shows as a rough spherical swelling on the stem, often near the crown; you have to pull the soil away from the stem to see it. Where one is found, remove the plant and burn it. Then remove the soil and replace it with clean soil. Prevention is best, so inspect all new plants coming into your garden and reject any that show galls. When galls are found on the roots, cut back to sound tissues; disinfect the knife after each cut.

A new material has recently been introduced which promises to help here. Test reports indicate that Bacticin will control galls.

*This is a nice solution to the problem of making an attractive
yet workable path. The gravel in the center takes care
of the heavy wear of the wheelbarrow, but the grass
sides show pleasing shades of green.*

NEMATODES

Until recently, nematodes were thought to be confined to the South and were considered no great threat to roses. Now we realize that we were wrong on both counts. Our knowledge of these almost microscopic animals (formerly called "eelworms") is increasing rapidly, and we find that a fair number of the many, many kinds can damage roses. If there is any question as to the possible presence of nematodes in your garden, take a soil sample, about a pint from several locations in the bed, and send it to the soil-testing laboratory at your state agricultural experiment station. (Use a plastic bag, as the soil must not dry out on the way.) If the report shows the presence of some of the bad ones (lance, dagger, meadow, root knot, and so on), control is not difficult. If the rose bed is just being made, and is not close to other desired plants, the soil can be treated with Garden Dowfume or D-D Mixture injected into the soil. In this case, four weeks should pass before planting. Where plants are growing use Nemagon, either as liquid or granules, or V-C13 Nematacide, at the rates given on the label.

ANIMAL PESTS

MICE

In some sections, mice are a particular hazard. As mentioned earlier, field mice will choose a winter mulch *put on before the ground is frozen* as winter quarters and will eat both bark and buds during severe weather. The pine mouse works entirely underground, feeding on roots, so it is difficult to identify and locate. Poisoned bait pushed into the runs and covered with a shingle, to protect pets, works well. Or a section of the run can be enlarged and a small mouse trap placed in it. A hard-working cat is the *ne plus ultra!*

MOLES

For years gardeners have tried many methods of killing moles—often at considerable expense and with limited success. Two fine controls are now available. Spray all your property (unless there is considerable acreage) with Chlordane—this kills the soil insects the moles are seeking. With no food supply in the area, the moles will go away. Or you can now buy an inexpensive gadget that attaches to the muffler of a power mower or a small tractor. The tube end is placed in the mole run and sealed with soil. After running the motor for a few minutes, the entire tunnel is filled with carbon monoxide and other unpleasant gases. *Fini!*

RABBITS AND DEER

Most of the damage to roses from these two pests comes during periods of severe weather, often with deep snow: the tips of the canes are eaten. Also, rabbits will winter in a fluffy mulch that is put on too early in the fall. The prime deterrent is a dog, a beagle or similar hunting type. Lacking that, there are repellents available (Sudbury, Ringwood, F. & B., and so on). You can use your own, with one or more ingredients—dried blood (renew often), naphthalene, or tobacco dust. After heavy snowfalls, repeat applications are called for. As a last resort, shotgun pellets (where legal) are effective—if well directed. If not, they can tear up a rose bush rather badly! For deer, use bullets of a caliber of not less than .30. Time of application—about dawn or twilight. (In cities and suburbs, forget it!)

THE GARDENER AS PEST

Dr. Cynthia Westcott has suggested—with considerable truth—that some gardeners are the worst pest their gardens have to endure. Sloppy handling of the hoe can leave damaged canes, which are an open invitation for a number of diseases—notably stem canker—and even some insects. Too deep cultivating damages roots, which tend to be very near the surface under a mulch. Using excessive amounts of fertilizer or putting it on dry soils can cause much damage. Excessive spraying damages the foliage—but, on the other hand, neglecting to spray according to a schedule can be nearly catastrophic. Leaving stubs when pruning or using dull tools is just asking for trouble. In other words, don't make a pest of yourself.

A FEW REMINDERS

Tack these on the toolshed wall.

1. With diseases it is *prevention* that counts—while there are leaves on the plants, protect them.

2. When spraying use only the specific materials needed at the moment. Multipurpose sprays are easy to use, but they add unnecessary chemicals to "the ecology" when only a single-purpose spray is needed.

3. Always use a sticker-spreader in spray mixtures—it gives better coverage and the sprays last longer. Dow and Ortho make good ones—in a pinch use Dreft.

4. Don't spray past the runoff point; it just wastes materials. Don't dust until the film is visible to the naked eye, but use a magnifying glass until you get the right amount—just the least possible amount to give good, if not visible, coverage.

5. Apply pesticides when there is little or no wind—this usually means early morning or late evening.

6. Dusts will stick to dry leaves as well as to those wet from dew or rain.

7. Timeliness is next to godliness in pest control. Early action reduces damage to a remarkable degree.

8. Read all of the label and follow directions to the letter!

9. Store spray and dust materials in a closet, locked if there are children around. Protect from extremes of heat and cold.

10. All discarded pesticides and containers should be sent to a "land fill" dump or buried at least 18 inches deep. Don't burn containers!

Chapter 8

Winter Protection—Where Necessary

Not all roses need winter protection. In areas where 0 degrees F. is the normal low, with a few minus degrees once in a while, most roses that have been well grown will come through nicely with no protection at all.

By eliminating this nasty two-part job, not only is the work load considerably reduced, but the plants are better off. By keeping the canes open to air and sun, the incidence of canker is greatly reduced. Where soil mounds or salt marsh hay are not solidly frozen during most of the winter, this disease can be very destructive.

If in doubt as to the necessity for some protection, run a test under *your* conditions. Protect some of your plants and leave some alone. In the spring, compare.

THE FIRST STEP: PROPER SELECTION

The heavy labor load of winter protection can be reduced greatly by the proper selection of the kinds of roses to be grown. If temperatures much below 10 degrees F.

are common, steer clear of most of the Teas, the Noisettes, and such tender Climbers as Lady Banksia, unless you plan to give them some winter covering. Most Hybrid Teas (but not all of the ones bred in England) will take −5 degrees F. with little damage. Most Hybrid Perpetuals, Floribundas, and Polyanthas are a bit more hardy. Many of the species and Shrub roses are even tougher; so, too, are many of the Old roses. Among the Climbers, the least hardy are the Climbing Hybrid Teas, then the Climbing Floribundas, the Repeat-Flowering Climbers, the Once-Flowering Climbers, and, finally, the Ramblers.

THE NEXT STEP: PROPER CULTURE

Even the hardiest rose can winter-kill if it is not in good health. A good, strong, well-hardened plant will need the least possible protection from winter's trials. Start in the spring and give the best culture you can. This, naturally, includes the best in pest control. Don't water, except in dire situations, after the early part of August. Six to eight weeks before hard frosts are expected, pull back the mulch so that the soil will dry out, preventing any more new growth. Where intense cold is expected, −10 degrees F. or lower, feed a no-nitrogen fertilizer, such as a 0–10–10, to hasten the hardening of the canes. This is not often sold at nurseries, but farm supply stores carry it as a "small grain" fertilizer.

SOIL MOUND PROTECTION

Most plants are protected by pouring soil into the center of the plant until a mound about eight to ten inches high has formed; this is enough for about −15 degrees F. For more extreme temperatures, plastic cones between 14 and 16 inches high are better; otherwise the canes will kill back to the soil line. Where such deep cones or

The classic winter protection
of a cone of earth covered with evergreen boughs
is effective—but entails a great deal of work.

mounds are called for, covering the whole surface with evergreen boughs is a good idea.

The soil used to make these mounds should have sharp drainage. It should not be scraped from the bed—the feeder roots near the surface would suffer. Bring the needed soil in from the vegetable garden or an annual bed—it can be returned in the spring.

In open winters, check the mounds from time to time, because rains can flatten them, reducing their effectiveness. Where high mounds are necessary, some kind of a collar should surround them. This can be made of roofing paper, fine mesh wire, plastic, or whatever comes to hand, and should be filled to the rim with soil. If these materials are not available, for the past five years or so there has been on the market a commercial strip, 12 inches high and 13 inches long, made of fiber glass over a supporting mesh. Another innovation comes in the form of a bottomless plastic box with a removable lid. These are gaining popularity very rapidly. One drawback is that the plants have to be pruned quite severely to fit inside.

In the most severe climates, and where regular-shaped beds are involved, many gardeners build a frame around the beds, form the soil mounds for each plant, and then build sides of insulating board or foam plastic insulating sheets. The whole box is filled with dry leaves, salt-marsh hay, or whatever is available of similar nature, and then the whole is covered with a top.

REMOVING THE PROTECTION

The mounds should not be left in place too long in the spring or soft new shoots will grow inside them. These will either be broken off when the soil is removed or the sun may burn them. In large gardens the work load can be spread out by taking

*Less soil or other material is needed for winter protection
where collars of roofing material
or other sheets are used, but the plants
have to be cut hard to fit.*

More and more plastics are being used—
both as films and sheets—
in one form or another in winter protection.

off the top of the mounds quite early and then removing the base just before pruning. The soil that is removed should be stockpiled in some out-of-the-way part of the garden, not just spread over the bed.

PROTECTING NONBUSH TYPES

RAMBLERS AND CLIMBERS

Ramblers need no protection except under the most severe conditions. Once-Flowering Climbers are, as a group, almost as hardy. Repeat-Flowering Climbers usually need protection against temperatures of –10 degrees F or less. Climbing Hybrid Teas and Floribundas benefit from protection against –5 degrees F. or less. The best way is to detach them from their supports early enough so that the canes are still fairly limber and lay them on the ground. Using wickets of stiff wire or X's of lath, pin them down. For a light cover, let the grass grow tall through and around them. In greater cold, cover them with soil. Trellises hinged near the ground speed up this chore, but some damage to canes must be expected. Where such measures are necessary, keep the older wood to a minimum when pruning.

TREE ROSES

A variation on the boxes built around beds is the new vertical box whose sides are made of weatherproof insulating foam. These surround the whole stem and head of the tree rose. Eleven bucketfuls of ground corncobs, or similar material, are dumped in and the top is fastened in place. This gives adequate protection down to –15 degrees F. Trying to grow tree roses in colder climates than that is just asking for hard work. The safest way is to dig up the plants and bury them in a trench. The plants

*Climbers are versatile—whether espaliered under the eaves,
framing the doors and windows, or softening the harshness
of the picket fence, they add color
and a softening grace.*

won't last long when given this treatment. They will last longer if you dig under one-half of the plant and then the stem and head are bent down into a trench and covered with soil. This isn't easy, and it takes up a lot of room. In moderate climates, such as Washington, D.C., trees budded on multiflora or rugosa stems can get by if you wrap the heads with burlap (green is nice) or heavy paper and enclose the whole in a large polyethylene bag.

It should be evident that any "low-labor" garden, except in the mildest areas, will have to get along without Tree roses.

Miniatures

The use of soil mounds to cover all or most of the plants is simple and easy here. Remove before growth starts in the spring.

THE NEED FOR WATER

No winter protection should ever be put on a dry soil. When the plant is well hardened and it is too cold for new growth, water thoroughly if necessary. Except under snow cover, water as necessary during the winter on *mild days only!*

Chapter 9

The Proper Tools

Having just the right tool for each job is not only good for the plants, but it makes the job easier as well. Too often gardeners make do with whatever comes to hand. However, while new tools are often sought to do a better job and make the work easier, some old, but relatively unknown, kinds are particularly suited to a rose-growing program.

HOES

Examples of the latter group lie in the mundane world of hoes. Most gardeners use an ordinary field hoe with a deep blade—and this mutilates or destroys countless surface roots every season. Damage to canes is also common where these unwieldy tools are used. And the shock of the chop-chop motion builds fatigue.

There are two hoes better designed for the now diminished (hallelujah!) chore of hoeing. The first is the onion or "nurseryman's" pattern, with a narrow and thin blade. After the chopping stroke, this can be *pulled* just under the soil surface, undercutting the weeds without hurting the roots of the roses. With one chop and pull as much area is covered as with six to eight chops using a field hoe.

Where beds are deep and stones are few, the Dutch scuffle hoe (better than the American pattern) with the long handle is a blessing. You can stand in front of the bed and do 90 percent of the hoeing from the front. This hoe is used with a push-pull motion, just under the surface of the soil. This means that the handle goes under the bush, with little chance of damaging the canes. With just a bit of practice, directional control is phenomenal, thus protecting the stems from damage.

PRUNING SHEARS

Poor pruning shears are an abomination—for both the plants and the gardener. They inflict crushed canes, which are slow to heal, on the plants and cramped hands on the gardener. Don't try for a bargain price—a good pair will last almost a lifetime if well cared for. New designs are light in weight, and have comfortable, plastic-covered handles and even Teflon-coated blades, which smooth the cut and reduce the necessary pressure. The Felco shear retains the long-used spring action; all parts are replaceable, including the extremely hard tool-steel blades. The Florian shear pictured employs a "ratchet action" for ease in making even big cuts, is very light in weight, and has Teflon-coated, stainless-steel blades.

One pair of hand shears is enough for many gardeners, but I like two. I always have a pair of grape-thinning shears (with straight, not curved, blades) in my pocket when working with roses. The very thin blades are unbeatable when it comes to cutting the excessive twiggy growth, especially with some Floribundas—and they are perfectly scaled for working with Miniature roses.

USEFUL GARDEN TOOLS
Illustrated overleaf

A. *If you grow more than about 50 plants this type of duster will handle the job; an attachment dusts two rows at a time.*

B. *The Atomist 1026 mister gives unparalleled coverage with a marked savings in spray materials but can be used only in range of an electrical outlet: good for a garden of 50 or more plants.*

C. *The "slide tube" duster is almost worthless for roses—it won't get to the underside of leaves —but may be adequate for a dozen or so plants or as emergency backup for other equipment.*

D. *A Florian ratchet-cut pruning shear which is "feather light," long lasting, almost rust proof, and easy on the cut.*

E. *The Dutch scuffle hoe is useful for cleaning the inside of deep beds but is not recommended for heavy or rocky soils.*

F. *The thin-bladed onion (or nurseryman's) hoe is fine for crowded plantings, but care is needed so that the bark is not injured.*

G. *This easy-to-use, lightweight duster is good for up to about 50 plants—especially for use between regular sprayings. An extension device is useful for the underside of leaves.*

H. *For heavy cuts the Florian lopping shear, mini or regular, uses a ratchet to give a clean cut.*

I. *A one-and-a-half gallon "Ladybug" sprayer for small plantings is light in weight and easy to clean.*

J. *A conventional "compression tank" sprayer comes in various capacities up to four gallons (the larger ones can be mounted on a two-wheeled cart) and is good for gardens of up to a hundred plants or more.*

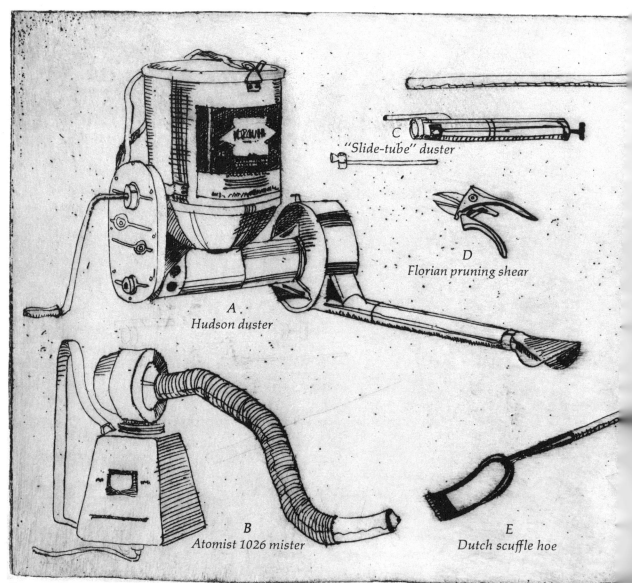

C
"Slide-tube" duster

D
Florian pruning shear

A
Hudson duster

B
Atomist 1026 mister

E
Dutch scuffle hoe

See preceding page for description of tools.

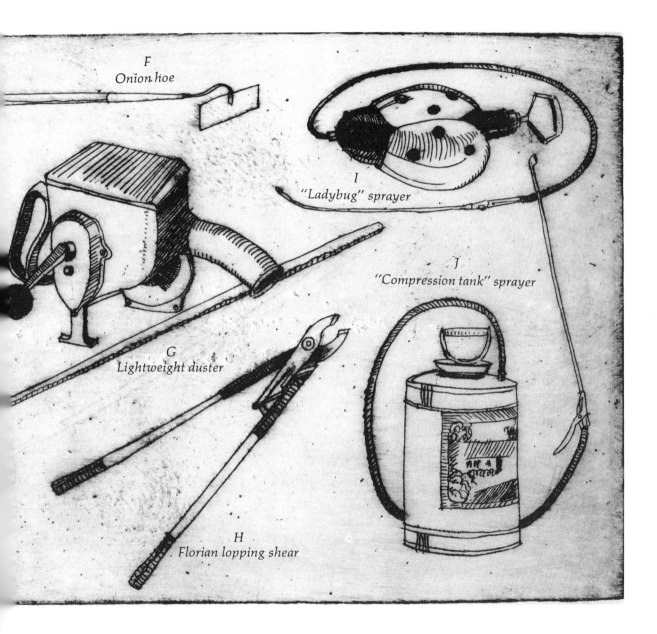

F
Onion hoe

I
"Ladybug" sprayer

J
"Compression tank" sprayer

G
Lightweight duster

H
Florian lopping shear

FOR THE BIG CUTS

If you try to cut a cane beyond the capacity of your hand pruner you are assured of a ragged cut, one that will invite disease and be slow to heal. Lopping shears are good for cuts up to an inch and a quarter; the oversized loppers (which cut to two inches) are too heavy. Look for Teflon-coated blades and cushioned handles on medium size loppers. Some have fiber glass reinforced handles and are lightweight, a positive factor where much heavy pruning is called for.

Where larger cuts are necessary—I measured the main stem of my Mary Wallace Climber this morning at better than two and three-quarters inches!—a small, curved-blade pruning saw should be used. Never use a saw with teeth on both edges —it will certainly cut into the bark of nearby canes. The new models with Teflon-coated blades won't bind, and are easy on the draw. Such saws can also be used on smaller canes, where the canes are so close that there isn't room for the lopper blades to operate without injuring the uncut cane. Saws are a necessity on the huge plants grown in some parts of the South and West, and on Climbers everywhere.

SPRAYERS

For small plantings (one to two dozen bushes) either forget spraying or use a "hose-end" sprayer. This doesn't give as fine a spray as is desired, but it can do a creditable job with the least fuss. Be certain to get a model with an extension nozzle, to allow the underside of the leaves to be covered. Those models with a shut-off valve are most convenient.

Those small (one quart or less) sprayers that spray only on the push stroke (intermittent) are worthless, while those which have continuous action are acceptable for small plantings if the nozzle can be turned to spray the underside of the leaves — but that requires more bending than I relish.

The "old faithful" for moderate to fairly large plantings is a "compression type" sprayer with a capacity of from two to four gallons. This is a tank that is carried with a strap over the shoulder. The smaller sizes are recommended for those with forty to fifty plants or for those who can't handle the weight of the larger sizes. The tanks can be made of galvanized iron, copper, or stainless steel. And since the three- or four-gallon tanks are quite heavy when they are filled, lightweight carts are now available to ease the load.

A whimsical, but practical, adaptation of this type of sprayer has been introduced as the "Ladybug." This sprayer, shaped and colored like its namesake, holds one and a half gallons, about enough for forty plants, in a plastic tank. Lightweight and easy to clean, it fills a gap between the small plunger-type sprayers and the large, heavy ones.

For large gardens, either the two-man-team wheelbarrow sprayers or the newer 10- to 30-gallon, motorized sprayers on wheels held the stage until a couple of years ago — and still do where electricity is not available. But in gardens where outside electrical outlets can be installed, it is now an entirely new ball game.

The new Atomist misters — scaled-down models of the monstrous machines used by orchardists, farmers, and nurserymen — give incomparable coverage. Small amounts of pesticides are fed into a large volume of air, which is propelled at tremendous force. The result is an all-enveloping mist that cloaks *all* surfaces — making complete control of pests possible. The pluses are many: savings on materials amount to 50 percent and more; in labor and time this can be as much as 80 percent! The smaller, one-and-a-half-gallon model will handle up to about 200 plants, and for larger gardens there is a five-gallon model mounted on wheels; when necessary the cart can be removed and the mister carried into position.

CARE OF SPRAYERS

The best of sprayers will do a poor job and have a short life unless it is well cared for. After each use it should be cleaned thoroughly. This means building up pressure and running the cleaning water through the wand and nozzle, then inverting for complete drying. A stout dowel set at a 45-degree angle in the tool-shed wall makes this easy and effective.

It is wise to keep a few nozzle disks and a pump leather on hand for emergencies. Too often these parts fail on a weekend, when no replacements are available. Check the fine nozzle disks frequently, for they wear and produce too-large droplets after a while.

When the season is over a complete cleanup is in order. Wash all metal parts in water liberally laced with washing soda; use a stiff-bristled brush vigorously — but not on the hose. With a stiff wire clean out the wand. Assemble the sprayer and partially fill with a water and vinegar mix. Build pressure and spray to clean the hose. Disassemble and dry thoroughly, then oil all metal parts and the leather washer on the pump. If necessary, replace the nozzle disk and the pump washer so that everything will be ready for spring.

DUSTERS

For small plantings the little rotary duster, with an extension nozzle to shoot the dust to the underside of the leaves, is very convenient. It is also useful for spot treatment in larger gardens, where spraying is the general rule. In larger gardens, with more than three or four dozen plants, a larger duster carried with an over-the-shoulder strap is called for. A duster like this can deliver either one or two streams of dust. The only care you need provide a duster is to oil the bearings from time to time and brush it out carefully before storing it for the winter. It might be mentioned that the "push-tube" dusters are an exercise in utter futility—besides being very expensive, per unit protected.

GLOVES

Too few gardeners give proper attention to gloves—and rose gardeners need the best. Fred Edmunds, Jr. (Box 68, Wilsonville, Oregon 97070), knows better. He has designed and had produced a glove especially for rose growers. These gloves are made of a special imported goatskin, with in-sewn seams. The water absorption is low, thorn resistance is high, and the gloves are smoothly flexible. Even ordinary gardeners appreciate them.

For dealing with massive Climbers, heavy leather gauntlets, such as welders use, are recommended.

Chapter 10

Roses in the Greenhouse

Growing Hybrid Teas and Grandifloras in the greenhouse for long-stemmed, large-flowered "florist roses" should be left to commercial growers. The amount of space needed and the fairly long time between "crops" make amateur production less than satisfactory.

The smaller cultivars of Floribundas, Polyanthas and the Miniatures are another matter, however, as they don't take up an excessive amount of room and are most attractive. They should be grown as pot plants—and they can yield a bonus in boutonnieres and small corsages.

Fairly large pots (ten inches or more) and tubs make suitable containers for the Floribundas and Polyanthas. The Miniatures usually require four- to six-inch pots, depending on the growth habits of the cultivars involved.

GROWING SCHEDULE

Buy the best-quality plants obtainable and pot them in November. A soil mixture of three parts good loam and one part well-rotted manure is fine. Some sharp sand should be added if the loam is even a bit heavy. If the manure is not available, use a coarse-grade peat moss. Add a cupful of superphosphate to each bushel of mix and half as much lime if the soil is on the acid side. Place the pots in a cold frame and mulch heavily in cold regions.

When the roots have made good growth (about January 1), bring the pots into the greenhouse, placing them under a bench. Cover with burlap, which must be kept moist. Inspect often, and when new shoots appear, shift to a sunny bench. A night temperature of 55 to 60 degrees F. is ideal, but a low of 50 degrees will do quite well. Watering must be ample, and a fairly high humidity (60 percent, more or less) and good ventilation are necessary for good growth. Feed every two weeks with a liquid fertilizer (about a 20–20–20), and spray as needed. Mildew can give considerable trouble, but Benlate should take care of that and any black spot which shows up. If aphides show, just spray with water; hard cases need Kelthane. When cutting blooms, leave as many leaves as possible on the plants; with the weak winter light all the food-producing capacity of the plant is important.

THE SUMMER PROGRAM

When late spring temperatures get too high, take the plants to a sunny spot in the garden and plant them to the rim if the pots are porous. Otherwise plant them out. Give them the same care as roses in the garden. When fall comes they should go back into the greenhouse—before any leaves fall—with no interruption in blooming.

MINIATURES IN THE GREENHOUSE

Miniature roses are especially suitable for such a program, especially where space is at a premium. They are very effective as house decorations when in peak bloom.

Keeping them in the house for long periods, however, is not recommended. The low light intensity and low humidity will slow growth and put an end to blooming. A good rule of thumb is to keep them in the house for a week and then return them to the greenhouse to recuperate.

RECOMMENDED VARIETIES

Usually the small-stemmed, low-growing Floribunda cultivars are best. Summer Snow, any of the Pinocchios, Garnet, Spartan, Gold Cup, Margo Koster, and Triomphe d'Orleans are all good. I haven't grown any of the more recent introductions under glass, but certainly all but the more vigorous ones would be suitable. In the Miniature group practically all varieties are adaptable, so selection can be made on preferences alone, based on the color, vigor, and habit of growth.

Chapter 11

Container Growing

WHY PLANT IN CONTAINERS?

Roses are grown in containers for two quite different reasons: for late planting and for ornamental purposes.

FOR LATE PLANTING

Each winter many thousands of roses are potted and brought into growth. In late spring and summer, when it is too late to plant bare-root plants, they are sold for immediate planting. Sometimes they are even in bloom—"instant roses"!

There is one drawback to such plants, however. As the container is of only moderate size, the roots are necessarily quite restricted in their spread. To make it worse, they seldom grow out of this tight pattern. If the plant is left in this fashion it will never make really normal growth, and its life span will be shortened.

The remedy is to grow the plant through the first season just as it is. When planting time comes with the next spring, dig the plant, untangle the roots carefully, and replant. By summer, growth should be entirely normal.

FOR ORNAMENTAL PURPOSES

For many years it has been common to grow roses in pots in the greenhouse, to take into the house or use as gifts when in bloom. Today there is an increasing tendency to grow more roses in large containers. These roses are generally grown in some out-of-the-way spot and then brought to the house, terrace, or porch when they are in bloom. These containers are not limited to the big, ugly clay pots of the past, but may be of plastic, cement, hand-formed clay, ceramic, or even redwood.

As some of these containers are of considerable size, larger-growing cultivars can be handled than in the past. And if these plants go out of bloom, they can be relegated to a nursery area until they come in again. During the winter these plants are usually planted directly in the ground and given the same protection as the roses in the garden. They can, however, be wintered in deep cold frames.

PREPARING THE CONTAINERS

Here, as in the garden, drainage is of prime importance. Adequate drain holes must be incorporated in all containers. In addition, a layer of pebbles or crock (broken pots) should be placed on the bottom. The most common, and probably the best, soil mixture consists of equal parts of good topsoil, either well-rotted manure or coarse peat moss, and really sharp, angular sand. If the latter is not available, use the horticultural-grade perlite or medium vermiculite. To each bushel of this add a pint of superphosphate. Some growers also add a pint of cottonseed meal.

PLANTING

These roses are planted in the spring. Follow the general planting rules as far as possible; roots will, of necessity, be somewhat cramped, so shorten them a bit. Do *not* follow the old-time rule of pounding the soil in with a hammer handle! Roses used to grow *in spite of* such treatment, rather than because of it. Just be sure the soil is firm around the roots and make certain that no air pockets remain. Feed every two weeks with liquid fertilizer and spray or dust as with garden roses.

Chapter 12

The Major Classes of Roses

All roses are classified in groups, each of which implies certain characteristics. This helps in making selections, but shouldn't be taken too literally—for crossbreeding has been going on for so long that the dividing lines are becoming increasingly blurred.

HYBRID TEAS

For 70 years or so Hybrid Teas have dominated rose growing—with good reason. From crosses between Hybrid Perpetuals and the true Tea roses, these newcomers, at the end of the last century, were hardier than the Teas, bloomed more frequently than the Hybrid Perpetuals, and had a better color range and more fragrance. Also, the Hybrid Teas gradually improved the flower form to the pointed bud that is desired today.

As time went on, other lines were brought in to improve the group. Probably the most important was the cross with Austrian Copper, although the profound influence of this is of the "good news–bad news" type. The color range broke out of the white-pink-crimson (low intensity, with bluish cast) rut. Then yellow, orange, and bright, clear scarlets, as well as blends, became possible. On the other hand, the low resistance to black spot was a very serious fault—although modern breeding programs are overcoming this to an increasing degree, as discussed in Chapter 7, Pest Control in Modern Terms.

With the advent of Grey Pearl (1944), the range was widened even further; this bloom is a soft gray-lilac. From that came Sterling Silver, with a delicate but haunting fragrance. Later came Twilight, a good lavender and pink, on a sturdier plant. Shades of buff or near-brown are also in the works.

Most Hybrid Teas are upright shrubs, from two to five feet high (more in the South and West). Large blooms open from pointed buds, generally one to a stem, although some cultivars tend to have cluster-blooms. Generally, they are a bit less hardy than the Hybrid Perpetuals and not quite as tall.

While Hybrid Teas are the equal of Floribundas in their adaptability *as a group*, there are a few exceptions to watch for. Burnaby is a lovely thing, with cream to light yellow flowers, but it does really well only on the West and East coasts. Fred Edmunds does best on the West Coast. Karl Herbst can be quite finicky.

The way around this, for the beginner, is to check with neighbors and friends. See as many nearby show gardens as possible. (See Appendix 2 for the location of the All-America Rose Selection Test Gardens.) Then check with your local nurseryman.

By all means, don't be snobbish in making your selections. The very latest introductions and the highest priced are not necessarily the best. Also, the top prize winners in rose shows may *not* be good garden plants.

Start with *proven cultivars* for the bulk of your beginning garden. Charlotte Armstrong (1940), Peace (1945), Golden Masterpiece (1953), and even Frau Karl Drushki (1900!) form the standard against which new roses are judged. And finally, don't forget fragrance when deciding which kinds to grow.

THE NEGLECTED SINGLES

All of the Hybrid Teas mentioned have double blooms, although some are more double than others. Most of the Hybrid Teas grown are double, which means that too many gardeners are missing some of the loveliest of all roses. The superb grace of the single-flowered sorts is pure delight, and the contrast between the petal colors and the stamens further enhances it. Not too many single Hybrid Teas are available, but every garden should have a few.

RECOMMENDED "STARTER" CULTIVARS

Recommending suitable, "fool-proof" cultivars is a hazardous occupation. If I were to include some of the newer kinds which have done well for me *before* the consensus has had time to be fully formed, they might prove to be only locally adapted. The only safe way out, for author *and gardener*, is for me to list only those kinds which have, for some time, been generally accepted as universally successful. Then the gardener with increasing knowledge and skill can make her or his own judgment of the more recent cultivars—and sort the poetic advertising blurbs from the realities. A bonus from such an approach is the money you will save in getting started.

Growing roses as Pillars
is not done as much as it should be—
they make dramatic accents.

TIME-TESTED HYBRID TEAS

The number after the name of a cultivar is the rating of the American Rose Society. This is based on the opinions of many thousands of society members in the United States and Canada, under all sorts of climatic and soil conditions. The ratings are expressed as numbers from 0 to 10, where 9.0 or more is outstanding, 8.0 to 9.0 excellent, 7.0 to 8.0 good, and 6.0 to 7.0 fair. You can just about forget those much below 7.0, except for special situations. These ratings are not to be considered infallible, but they are a helpful guide as to the *garden worthiness* of the various cultivars.

BLANCHE MALLERIN 6.4

Good whites are scarce, so treasure this. The long, urn-shaped buds are lovely, and the open flower is well formed and has a wonderful fragrance.

CHAMPAGNE 7.9

A pale buff-yellow color flushed with a hint of apricot, which does well in heat. It is a vigorous plant, but not too hardy.

⅄ CHARLOTTE ARMSTRONG 8.4

Magnificent color and form, much used in breeding superior new kinds. Plenty of big, deep rose-pink blooms on a husky plant, and they are fragrant. A must in any garden.

CHICAGO PEACE 8.4

Has all the vigor and big, healthy foliage of her famous parent, but has a richer flush of pink over a coppery-yellow base color.

CHRYSLER IMPERIAL 8.9

A fine crimson that blooms heavily, regardless of heat, cold, rain or whatever! It is wonderfully fragrant, but watch the mildew.

CONFIDENCE 8.4

The all-over pink has golden tones in shapely, exhibition-type blooms, which are nicely fragrant.

DIAMOND JUBILEE 7.0

The high-centered blooms are buff-yellow—and they don't fade in heat. The plant is especially vigorous, and also quite hardy.

FORTY-NINER 6.1

Why the low rating? The plant is not the best—but the bicolor blooms are unique. They are a deep buff-crimson with an old-gold reverse, if that means anything. See it and you will agree. A plant or two will be enough, but try it—you'll like it!

GARDEN PARTY 7.9

The creamy yellow blooms have a "frosting" of pink at the edges of the petals. Although very free flowering, wet weather slows it down; best in the fall.

HELEN TRAUBEL 8.3

She is not for exhibition, but for an almost never-ending supply of pink and apricot blooms for garden display and cutting; delightfully fragrant. The plant is vigorous.

KING'S RANSOM 7.6

The large, well-shaped, golden-yellow blooms are freely produced in all weathers, and they do not fade. The dark, glossy leaves are on vigorous plants.

KORDES' PERFECTA 7.6

Some consider this too old, but it is a lovely, huge pink, with carmine markings giving it a sparkle—especially in light shade and in the fall.

MCGREDY'S YELLOW 6.1

This is an easy to grow, disease-resistant plant with lemon-yellow blooms that contrast nicely with the reddish foliage and huge (wicked!) red thorns.

MICHELE MEILLAND 7.9

The blooms are pink, and in cool weather show some salmon. The size is medium, but the form is impeccable. The plant is a vigorous grower—don't let the "refined look" fool you.

MIRANDY 7.1

It is a mistake to plant this in a cool, moist climate, but it is a fine, *deep* burgundy-red for warmer, drier locations. The high-centered, very double blooms are strongly fragrant. The plants are on the low side, about two and a half feet, and quite dense.

MISTER LINCOLN 8.4

All too few reds have good, sturdy, disease-resistant plants that produce plenty of blooms. This one does. The deep crimson blooms are a bit flatter than most modern Hybrid Teas.

MME. HENRI GUILLOT 7.1

This is really reaching back (1938), but I love the brilliant combination of coral, orange, and red in the beautifully formed blooms—it is unique. The plant is good.

MOJAVE 7.6

The fairly large blooms have a striking combination of coppery-orange with red tints. The deepest color is found in light shade and in the fall. The petals have a heavy substance and form a high-centered bloom, which is fragrant.

PAPA MEILLAND 7.7

A vigorous, easy plant with plenty of velvety crimson blooms, which are very fragrant. A good exhibition rose.

PASCALI 8.3

Pure white, medium-sized, fragrant blooms in abundance—a fantastic score for a white! Its disease-resistant foliage and great vigor are also major pluses.

PEACE 9.4

Possibly the top Hybrid Tea of this century. A big vigorous plant well covered with large, rich green, glossy foliage. The huge blooms mix cream and gold, then add pink at the petal edge. A landmark in Hybrid Teas.

PICTURE 7.6

Old (1932) but a very lovely, small pink. Plant closer than normal, about two feet or less in hard climates. The leaves are dark green and glossy. It has a tendency to rest a bit in summer, but it is still hard to beat.

PINK PEACE 7.7

This is not up to the standard of its famous parent—but then, what is? It is vigorous, disease resistant, and has big, rich pink flowers—which are slightly fragrant. (Peace's aren't.)

PRIMA BALLERINA 7.9

A very fragrant, medium size, rose-pink with tints of carmine. Freely produced, even in damp, cool weather. The foliage is dark green and glossy.

SOUTH SEAS 7.9

The rather spreading plants have reddish foliage. The rich, shell-pink buds open to a soft salmon (coral) pink of huge size and matchless form. Vigorous but not too hardy.

SUMMER SUNSHINE 7.6

Pure, bright gold in elegant form and free blooming habit. The blooms contrast well with bronzy foliage on a tall and robust plant.

SUTTER'S GOLD 7.8

Tall and vigorous, but the foliage is on the skimpy side. The sharply pointed buds open into medium yellow blooms with a red flush on the outer petals. Does best in hotter climates, but bloom size goes down in heat. The fragrance has an intense, fruity aroma.

TIFFANY 9.1

If you like *long* stems, here they are, bearing long, pointed buds opening to large blooms of deep pink with a touch of gold at the base of the petals. The fragrance is lovely, the plant tall and vigorous.

VIRGO 6.8

Don't let the rating put you off. Pure white color, vigor, and good disease resistance are not so common that you can afford to pass up one as good as this. When you add nicely formed blooms, and plenty of them and good fragrance as well, this is worth growing anywhere.

THE "BLUES"

When "blue" Hybrid Teas first showed up, growers fell sharply into two camps—the pros and the cons. The latter just said flatly that blue was not a suitable color for a rose. The pro group, however, saw Grey Pearl as a most valuable color break —and they were right. Good progress is being made in the lavender, lilac, and "blue" portions of the spectrum, but the group is so new that seasoned judgments are few.

GREY PEARL 4.0

Although this may have more historical than garden interest, the beautifully formed, pale lavender-gray blooms are lovely. The bush seldom reaches three feet.

STERLING SILVER 5.9

Less than vigorous, with well-formed blooms, the softest of lilac and silver-gray, this has a haunting fragrance that should be cherished.

Of the more recent kinds, not yet fully tested under all conditions, here are a few that look quite promising:

BLUE MOON 7.6

A real lavender, with good, pointed buds. Opens a nice lilac, with little fading.

INTERMEZZO 5.5

Like so many, a "silvery color," lavender in this case, on a rather short plant.

LADY X 8.1

Even those with reservations about "blue" roses will love this pale lavender. The vigorous, attractive plant grows to seven feet, with disease-resistant foliage. The blooms are slightly fragrant.

SILVER STAR

This is too new to have any rating, but the blooms have a lovely, soft lilac-blue color. The hardy plant has foliage that is quite disease resistant.

THE LOVELY SINGLES

Not too many single-flowered Hybrid Teas are available, but some should be in every garden.

CECIL 7.2

Five large, butter-yellow petals from a long, slender bud. The plant is vigorous.

DAINTY BESS 8.3

The best known single has five "fluted" petals of light pink with just a hint of lilac. This contrasts beautifully with the throng of golden stamens. No other single-flowered Hybrid Tea is hardier. There is a climbing form.

IRISH FIREFLAME 6.5

The flame color is in the bud, which opens lighter, with a flush of gold. The plant is modest in size—from three to four feet. Surely this rates a higher score!

WHITE WINGS 7.3

The very pointed buds open pure white, in beautiful contrast to the red stamens. They are fragrant. The plant is vigorous and fairly hardy.

THE SUB-ZERO HYBRID TEAS

Perhaps these should be in the main list, but here they can be treated as a special group and their special attributes emphasized. Dr. Brownell had two main goals in his breeding of these roses: cold hardiness and disease resistance. The following kinds all have these two traits, making them especially good for severe climates, although they grow well everywhere.

ARCTIC FLAME 6.5

This has large, well-shaped, bright red blooms on vigorous plants.

CURLY PINK 7.6

The large, fully double blooms are two-toned pink, and the petals recurve when the bloom is fully open.

DR. BROWNELL 7.3

While this is usually listed as a medium yellow, it does have tints of orange in the center.

HANDSOM RED 5.7

One of the early kinds, a deeper (bluer) red than Arctic Flame.

HELEN HAYES 7.1

The opening flower is rich yellow, which takes on a slight pink flush and orange tones as it develops. The vigorous plant is nearly thornless. The fragrance is good.

QUEEN O' THE LAKES 7.7

The velvety red blooms are not as fully double as the others, so the golden stamens add a nice contrast. This is fragrant, too.

RED DUCHESS 7.6

The large plants have rose-carmine blooms, which are more fragrant than others in the group.

FLORIBUNDAS

For more than a decade the dominance of the Hybrid Teas has been increasingly threatened by the ever-more popular Floribundas. But, whimsically, it doesn't much matter any more. The Floribundas came into being as hybrids between Polyanthas, some Hybrid Polyanthas, and Hybrid Teas. Ever since, they have depended more and more on the Hybrid Tea influence to give larger flowers with high-pointed buds, fewer cluster-flowers, and sturdier canes. Now, with many of the new cultivars, the line between the two classes is becoming ever more blurred. It is important, when planning a garden, to differentiate between the light-caned, small kinds and the heavy-caned, strong-growing kinds.

These shrubs, which vary from slightly more than 18 inches to 5 feet, are quite hardy and vigorous. They are seldom without some bloom, and generally they bear masses. The flowers may be borne in clusters, or may be one to a stem—or a combination of both. There are proportionately more Floribundas with single or semidouble flowers than in the Hybrid Teas. Fragrance varies quite widely and is generally low. The color range is widening here, too, with Angel Face, a rich lilac-lavender with semidouble flowers, among the notable new ones.

SOME PROVEN GOODIES

Trying to pick just a few Floribundas that have been widely proven is a thankless task, for all experienced growers will immediately add their favorites and take out some that they, personally, don't like—perhaps because of some prejudice of color or form. In the light of this, here are my recommendations:

ANGEL FACE

It is really too early to call this one "established," but the richly colored lilac blooms, with the golden stamens showing in the semidouble flowers, is a trailblazer. The bush is not very high, and the leaves are of medium size.

BETTY PRIOR 9.0

If you have read this far, you know I am in love with her—and so are millions of others. Vigorous and tall, she bears seemingly endless single carmine-pink flowers, lighter inside, with a slight fragrance. This hardy plant should be in every garden. Don't count on the "usual height, four feet," as she is robust!

CIRCUS PARADE 7.6

This may turn out to be an improvement on the parent Circus (8.0). A bit of apricot in the yellow coloring brightens it a bit.

ELIZABETH OF GLAMIS 7.6

Large but slender buds open salmon-pink, with glints of light orange. She is delightfully fragrant.

EUROPEANA 8.3

This one is fine for bedding, as it is low growing and has masses of dark red flowers. The foliage is bronzy and the plant very hardy. The fragrance is slight.

"Trelliage" is almost forgotten in modern gardens—
a pity. It can be designed to fit any style
and just begs for roses—often combined with clematis—
to soften hard architectural lines.

FASHION 8.0

Rather far from new, but will still take a lot of beating. The beautifully formed blooms are a sparkling combination of orange and salmon, and they appear constantly; they are fragrant. The plant is bushy and low. Ivory Fashion (8.0) differs only in color.

FRENSHAM 8.2

The large, arching canes produce a wealth of deep red blooms all season long; they, too, are fragrant. The plants are vigorous and hardy. This makes a wonderful hedge plant.

GINGER 8.2

A low, spreading plant with pure orange flowers in small clusters. These hold their color well in hot sun, and wet, cool weather doesn't stop them.

ICEBERG 8.5

The small, pure white, and beautifully formed blooms are borne in small clusters on a big plant. The medium green, glossy, disease-resistant leaves look like holly.

LAVENDER GIRL 7.0

The large, fragrant, pinky-lavender blooms are deeper in hue than most; they come from ruby-red buds. The plant is spreading and low, with dark green leaves.

LAVENDER PINOCCHIO 5.7

This is grown mainly for its unique color, lavender, with yellowish-buff tones. It is a strong-growing plant that blooms freely. It should have a far better rating than this.

I
Informal plantings can be enjoyed
by you and your neighbors.
Here the Hybrid Tea Roman Holiday
brightens a whole neighborhood.

II
This Climber City of York
makes a lovely screen planting,
with the Tree rose adding
a spot of color for accent.

III
There is no better way to tie the garden
to the house than by using Climbers.
This is the old-timer Mary Wallace;
she is still good, but blooms only once.

IV
The Musk Rose Hybrids are Shrubs, but the species carries
its single, pure white blooms, centered with golden stamens,
in a dazzling display twenty feet or more high,
filling the air with its "musky" fragrance.

V

Belinda, Hybrid Musk, is a prime, modern Shrub rose—
with lowest possible maintenance. The small, bright pink flowers
are borne in big trusses all summer long.
Musks will thrive in more shade than most roses will tolerate.

VI
Climbing roses are more versatile than the name implies.
Climbing Tom-Tom is a case in point: at the left
it is grown as a Climber and on the right as a free-standing Shrub.
Some can even be grown as ground covers.

VII
There are also many uses for Shrub roses in any landscape plan—
and not all of them for tall hedges or screening.
Sea Foam, vigorous and free-blooming,
shows one such use.

VIII
Large formal gardens appeal to many and give a great deal of pleasure.
These older Hybrid Teas, Crimson Glory and Mrs. P. S. Du Pont,
are in the rose garden of Longwood Gardens,
Kennett Square, Pennsylvania.

LILAC CHARM 7.8

The charm and grace of the single, pale lilac blooms is lovely. The plant is low, but vigorous and hardy.

LITTLE DARLING 8.6

The well-shaped little blooms are a soft pink, with an apricot flush. They are borne in clusters fine for cutting, on long, arching canes. The plant is hardy, vigorous, and quite disease resistant.

MASQUERADE 7.6

This strong, hardy plant is constantly covered with yellow flowers, which change as they age. The second phase puts on a flush of salmon and pink, then the whole bloom turns red; all three can be found on the plant at one time.

ORANGEADE 8.3

The single, orange-gold blooms are mainly borne in huge clusters on bushy plants. The color is so bright it almost shouts.

PINK CHIFFON 7.4

When a very soft pink is needed, this one is hard to beat, with plenty of blooms on a low but vigorous plant.

REDGOLD

This is too new to be proven (or have a rating), but it looks like a big winner. The large blooms are golden, with a flush of rich scarlet on the edges of the petals, spreading deeper into the bloom as it ages. The plants are big and husky.

The old Ramblers are still seen
in much of the Northeast,
often entirely covering an old stone wall.

ROSENELFE 7.9

This is often grown for cutting only, as the soft pink blooms look like little camellias and last well.

SARABANDE 7.9

The single to semidouble flowers have been described as "dazzling crimson," and they are constantly produced in small to large clusters. The plant is spreading in habit.

SARATOGA 7.7

Good whites are scarce, but this one has large, fully double flowers in good numbers, regardless of the weather.

SPARTAN 8.4

Beautifully formed coral buds open salmon-orange, with a delightful fragrance. The plants are of medium size and vigorous. There is a climbing form, and both are free blooming.

SUMMER SNOW 7.7

The bush form has been outdated by Iceberg, but the climbing form is good in itself or as a weeping Tree rose.

VOGUE 8.2

Beautifully formed, pure pink flowers all season long; they are larger than those of her sister seedling, Fashion. The plant is vigorous, and the leaves have a purple tinge.

GRANDIFLORAS

This newest group is a direct result of the recent blurring of the line between Hybrid Teas and Floribundas, discussed above. Some rose enthusiasts doubt the need for the group, and I tend to agree.

As a whole, cultivars in this group are vigorous to six feet, quite hardy, and very free flowering. The blooms may be one to a stem or moderately cluster flowered.

AMONG THE BEST

The group is quite new, so there are not too many to recommend, but there are some real beauties!

CAMELOT 8.2

A lovely coral (salmon?) pink in very heavy clusters. The plants are large, to seven feet, and vigorous. The foliage is big and quite disease resistant.

CARROUSEL 8.4

The deep red blooms have only 20 petals but are lovely, with a nice fragrance. Prolonged heat will cut blooming somewhat. Some blooms are one to a stem, others in clusters. The plant is not as tall as most.

MONTEZUMA 8.6

The bud is short, but the pinky-salmon bloom is high-centered, with about 40 petals. In cool or damp weather the color becomes pinky-coral. The plant is tall and big, so give it enough room.

MOUNT SHASTA 8.0

The slender buds open pure white. The early flowering is on the light side, but the big, disease-resistant plants make up for this in late summer and fall. Few whites have such a high rating.

QUEEN ELIZABETH 9.3

There is no doubt—queen of the group! The plant is vigorous, tall, and disease resistant. The medium-sized flowers are "middle pink" (one to several per stem) and appear constantly. The one fault is that there is little fragrance.

SCARLET KNIGHT 8.0

Not as tall as some, but has dark, glossy green foliage that is quite disease resistant. The canes are heavy, and the thorns murderous! The dark crimson blooms have a velvety sheen; they are borne one to a stem sometimes, but usually several. The fragrance is nice and plentiful.

Chapter 13

Climbing Roses

No rose is actually a Climber—roses have no holdfasts, tendrils, or other means of attachment. Their more or less limber canes range from 8 feet to more than 50, the longer ones going up simply by overwhelming any available support.

Here again, the lines of classification are too fuzzy for exact grouping. Blossom-time is rated as a Climber to about eight feet; I prefer to raise it as a graceful shrub growing about six feet. Many of the taller Shrub roses make excellent Pillars.

On the other hand, Climbing Sports (mutations) of smaller bush cultivars, such as Cl. Dainty Bess, leave no doubt as to where they belong.

The type of support given will be determined by the landscape style of the garden as well as the growth habit of the plant involved.

WHY NOT TRY SOMETHING DIFFERENT?

Climbing roses are usually grown on trellises, arbors, fences, walls, and arches. They are sometimes grown as espaliers on walls of buildings. But, unfortunately, very few gardeners grow them on supports that are available in many gardens. Even though roses are not true climbers, they will clamber over trees quite readily and make notable pictures!

Old, gnarled apple trees, as well as many of the larger crab apples, make fine supports. You can think of many others—but stay away from those with a dense habit of growth. Rose species or cultivars can be selected to match the size of the trees. For best results, the trees used should have fairly low branching, to keep the blooms somewhere near eye level. Be certain to select roses that are quite disease resistant, to cut down on maintenance. The fact that the leaves are far above the soil is already a step in that direction, for they are above the "normally infected zone."

RAMBLERS

Ramblers are not as popular as they used to be, except where the winters are really severe and a minimum of winter fuss is the rule. As an example, from the 1920s through the 1940s my family had a summer home in southern New Hampshire. We arrived in early June and left on Labor Day. It was impossible to do anything at all to protect the Dorothy Perkins and Crimson Ramblers. Yet in a few years they became a jungle over the long arbor across the whole front of the house and around to the side porch. Usual winter temperatures went to –20 to –25 degrees F., and sometimes went lower. We just cut out what winterkill we could reach in June— never more than 10 percent. Be warned, however—Dorothy Perkins can bring in mildew, even when there doesn't seem to be any around. The canes grow to about 20 feet, and are quite pliable. They make a great show of large clusters of small blooms, sometimes repeating a little.

When a fence is called for,
why settle for the plain old picket type?
This delicate design enhances the beauty
of the roses growing on it.

CLUSTER-FLOWERED RAMBLERS

AMERICAN PILLAR 7.4

This is a misnomer, as the plants will grow to 20 feet. The single flowers are rose-pink with a white center, and are carried in large clusters.

CHEVY CHASE 8.1

"An improved Crimson Rambler" with small, double, rose-carmine blooms in large clusters.

CRIMSON RAMBLER 6.7

Large clusters of small, bright crimson blooms last for about a month. Very hardy, and less subject to mildew than Dorothy Perkins. The "fragrance" comes from the *R. multiflora* parent, and is not too pleasant.

DOROTHY PERKINS

The small, double, light pink flowers are borne in many, many clusters for about a month in June and July; they have some fragrance. She mildews very badly, but otherwise is so rugged that she has "gone wild" in many areas. She makes a fine ground cover.

TAUSENDSCHÖN

This thornless plant is not as vigorous as the two above by half; ten feet is the usual limit. Neither is it as hardy. The enormous clusters of blooms vary from pink to almost white.

VEILCHENBLAU

This is not a recommendation—it is a warning. The metallic blue to maroon blooms are nauseous—but some "fly-by-night" dealers claim that this is the first blue rose. Forget it!

VIOLETTE

This is an improved Veilchenblau, with pure violet, semidouble flowers. It is worth growing for the color alone.

Large-Flowered Ramblers

This is the new name for the old "Once-Flowering Climbers." Most of the cultivars in this group have medium to fairly large flowers of better form, which are borne in quite loose clusters. Some, like Mrs. Arthur Curtiss James, bear a single large flower per stem—a lateral from older wood.

The group includes some fine cultivars, even if they only bloom once. They make big plants with strong canes, much stouter than the Ramblers. Most of them are slightly less hardy than the Ramblers (as a group)—but there is a trap here. Some few are the result of crosses, including the more tender Cherokee rose or *R. gigantea*. As a rule, these are not hardy north of Philadelphia or Long Island. The rule, however, is broken by the very lovely Kitty Kininmonth. She is hardy enough to grow in Boston.

Practically all of these have good disease resistance—Dr. Van Fleet and Silver Moon are typical—and all of these plants get big. They are not for lightweight trellises, so plan accordingly. It doesn't help much to prune heavily, for it is on short laterals of the older wood that the blooms are borne.

DR. VAN FLEET 8.7

Why this is still planted is a mystery to me, for he sported New Dawn—which repeats. In June, however, the shell-pink flowers make a real show and give off a delicate fragrance. Very vigorous and hardy.

KITTY KININMONTH 7.5

This is the hardiest of the Ramblers with *R. gigantea* in its breeding. The large, cupped, semidouble, nonfading pink blooms are quite fragrant. With that breeding it is natural that she is very vigorous, but where the sometime-repeat blooming comes from isn't clear.

MARY WALLACE 7.8

The large, semidouble, medium pink blooms really cover the vigorous plant. It is said to repeat at times, but mine never has. The blooming period, however, lasts for weeks. She will grow for years with no care; the leaves will show a little black spot, but she seems to shrug it off. Fine for growing in a large tree.

PAUL'S SCARLET 8.3

This is still offered, but can't really compete with the "New Blaze," which repeats very well.

SILVER MOON 7.8

The buds are yellow, but the fairly large, semidouble flowers are creamy-white. The slightly fragrant blooms come in large clusters on a plant as vigorous as Mary Wallace. Quite disease resistant.

THOR 7.3

It only blooms once, but you should put it in a tree for its huge, fully double, fragrant, dark red blooms. Very hardy and very disease resistant.

CLIMBERS

What were formerly called "Recurrent Climbers" hold a big place in the whole rose picture. They are quite big plants, have large—and often beautifully formed—blooms in astonishing numbers, and make a blaze of color at the beginning of the season, some during the summer, and more again in the fall. On the whole they are only a little less hardy than the Large Ramblers. They grow and bloom beautifully, without winter protection, in all the fairly mild regions of the country. Naturally, they are widely popular. In addition, with some protection they can encroach on the more severe climates, where the once-blooming kinds are more common. But don't undertake much protection lightly; these plants are quite large, and with age the canes become hard to handle.

A good number of recommendations are made in other chapters, especially in The Species and Shrub Roses (Chapter 15) and Roses from Grandmother's Garden (Chapter 16).

ALOHA 6.8

This Pillar has large, rose-pink blooms of impeccable form.

BLAZE 7.9

Be certain to get the "improved" form, which repeats much better than the first introduction. This is really a Pillar, as it seldom grows more than eight feet high. It bears a constant procession of rich, red blooms.

BLOSSOMTIME 7.8

This is low for a Climber, to eight feet, and as I said before, I prefer it as a shrub—if you have the room. Either way, it is a constant delight, with its salmon-pink—with a deeper reverse—beautifully formed blooms, which are delightfully fragrant. The late "Buck" Thorne, one-time president of the Men's Garden Club of America, had this as a shrub by his front door. He had a standing bet that no one could come to his home from early June to November and find this bush out of bloom. He never lost on this bet—even if he was a lousy poker player!

CORAL DAWN 7.6

This cluster-flowered plant has large, well-formed, coral-pink blooms. The disease-resistant plant seldom tops ten feet. Love that color!

DON JUAN 8.1

I rated this, under a coded number before it was named, for the AARS in the Test Garden of Biltmore Gardens and could not believe the amount of bloom in a hot and dry summer. The fully double, fairly large blooms are deep red and appear constantly. The plants are not big, seldom eight feet, but they are vigorous and hardy. They took –7 degrees with no protection—and with no winterkill. Red isn't my favorite color, but I love this one.

DREAM GIRL 6.7

A lovely blend of pink and salmon, in fully double, fragrant blooms all season long. She needs good culture for best results. Keep phosphorus high to prevent floppy necks.

Climbers treated as espaliers
are to be preferred to blanketing a whole wall;
caring for them is much easier this way.

HIGH NOON 7.0

A good yellow Pillar—but not for severe climates.

INSPIRATION 7.8

A beautifully formed, very large, semidouble pink with an out-of-this-world fragrance. Tops out at about eight feet, but is vigorous and hardy.

MORNING DAWN 7.2

Here is another rose with leaves like holly. The light pink flowers are large, beautifully formed, and fragrant. A Pillar to eight feet.

NEW DAWN 8.4

This recurrent sport from Dr. Van Fleet has the same fragrant, double, shell-pink flowers, which fade on aging. It was sensational in its day, but better ones are now here.

PARADE 7.9

This one has a crisp, rose-carmine bloom with good fragrance. The blooms are moderate in size. A Pillar to ten feet.

SPECTACULAR 7.5

The color is an orange-red, and the double blooms are borne in clusters; it repeats well. The height is only seven feet.

TEMPTATION 7.3

The fragrant, carmine blooms appear continuously.

CLIMBING HYBRID TEAS AND FLORIBUNDAS

When the bush form of any of these sports a Climbing plant, it will not be quite as hardy as the parent. This is only natural, for more of the plant is exposed to the rigors of winter. In areas where the canes of the parent *require* a soil mound to save the plant, forget the Climbing form—unless the whole is to be taken down and covered. As most of these have more pliable canes than those in the classes described above, and the full bulk of the plant is less, a limited number can well be grown without too great a work load for winter protection.

The main advantage of cultivars in these groups is that they produce far more blooms in a limited amount of space than do their bush counterparts. They are also useful from the standpoint of garden design, making it possible to have taller plantings at the back, to act as a background.

Those who prefer the classic bloom form will choose among the Climbing Hybrid Teas, but for almost uninterrupted masses of color the Climbing Floribundas are hard to beat, even though the blooms are smaller. As a group they are hardier.

A FEW RECOMMENDED CLIMBING HYBRID TEAS

CL. CHRISTOPHER STONE 6.7

A good red.

CL. CRIMSON GLORY 7.7

Much hardier than most. Rich red, velvety, and strongly fragrant.

*Changes of level can be most attractive
in any landscape. Here Climbers are
carefully restrained to accent the wall.*

X **CL. DAINTY BESS 8.2**

All the charm of the bush form on a much bigger scale. Single, salmon-pink, with a silvery sheen.

CL. MRS. SAM MC GREDY 8.2

A lovely orange blend with good form.

CL. NOCTURNE 7.3

A fine dark red.

CL. PEACE 7.3

When this first came out the demand was so great that some growers used every bud they could see. This resulted in plants of widely differing quality. Some were covered with bloom and some were sparse. Check the source before buying. One of the hardiest of all.

CL. PICTURE 7.8

A classic pink.

CL. SUTTER'S GOLD 7.9

Deep yellow, touched with red.

MRS. WHITMAN CROSS 7.4

The semidouble blooms are orange-apricot and are borne in clusters all season long.

GOOD CLIMBING FLORIBUNDAS

CL. GOLDILOCKS 5.7

Clear yellow, nice form, and fragrant.

CL. PINKIE 7.6

Clear pink.

CL. SUMMER SNOW 7.6

Clusters of small, white blooms, which are fragrant. Bloom is continuous.

CL. WORLD'S FAIR 7.5

A good red.

LESS HARDY CLIMBERS

The Climbing Teas will be mentioned in the chapter on Old roses (Chapter 16), but there are three whose names are thoroughly woven into the romance of the South. All are tender, but the first two are more so than Lady Banksia. Maréchal Niel (Noisette) is famous for his large, double, yellow, very fragrant blooms. The stems are weak, so plant where it will be natural to look up into them. The cut blooms last well, and the blooming season is long. It is a gamble to plant this where more than a little frost is to be expected. Even less hardy is Lamarque (another Noisette), but here the yellow color is softer—from light yellow to creamy-white. The weak necks and rich fragrance are proof of the Tea side of his ancestry.

Lady Banksia is quite another matter. This very vigorous, almost (sometimes entirely) thornless plant is considerably hardier. Near Greenville, South Carolina, ten years ago, a huge plant endured 0 degrees F. with no apparent damage. The blooms start early, February in the Deep South, and last for a long time. They are almost tiny, but in such great numbers that it doesn't matter. The two most popular kinds are the double white, which is quite fragrant, and the prettier double yellow,

There are few ground covers better than roses— if the proper kinds are selected.
Kept confined or allowed to cover open stretches of ground,
they are colorful, easy to grow, and smother almost all weeds.

which isn't. I believe that this could be planted considerably further north than is generally attempted.

Probably another fairly tender yellow-flowered cultivar should be added—Mermaid (hybrid *bracteata*). Possibly as hardy as Lady Banksia, Mermaid has single, large, pale yellow flowers, which are sparingly recurrent. The leaves are quite attractive. But unless you have a great deal of room or are willing to prune the stout canes, with their *very* stout thorns, severely, you may run out of room. Perhaps it is best used to cover a whole wall—such as a garage—and one plant will do it.

CREEPERS

This is not a recognized group or classification, just a grouping by a use not often enough employed in most gardens. Some roses make fine ground covers and some, the less rampant kinds, are fine to brighten a rock outcropping. For such use they must be hardy, vigorous in growth—to suppress the weeds—and quite disease resistant. Of course, the size, color, and frequency of their bloom, and how attractive their fruits are, have a bearing also.

Two very good and well-known kinds are *R. wichuraiana* and Max Graf. Both of these are quite vigorous, hardy, and quite resistant to diseases. The former has single, white blooms, which are a bit fragrant and borne in panicles. The hips are small and bright red. It blooms but once. Max Graf is a result of a cross between this and *R. rugosa*, so is even hardier and has somewhat larger, pink flowers. Where the soil is sandy and where salt spray can be counted on, this can only be equaled by *R. rugosa repens alba*. The flowers of the latter are white, followed by red fruits. Under better conditions both of these Rugosas will do even better; in dry soils water them at least until they are well established.

While Walter Brownell was working on his Sub-Zero Hybrid Teas, he carried on another, parallel project. From this came his Ground-Cover Series, all from *R. wichuraiana* on one side of the crosses. They have all of the hardiness, disease resistance, and a bit less of the vigor of that parent. On the other hand, they have a wide range of color, and some even repeat in bloom. Carpet of Gold, double yellow and fragrant, and Creeping Everbloom, fragrant, double red, are recurrent—the latter just about continuous. Little Compton Creeper not only has single, deep pink flowers, but conspicuous orange fruit. Coral Creeper fades from apricot to pink, but my favorite is Magic Carpet, which carries blooms of orange, yellow, and carmine—much like Masquerade among the Floribundas.

A WORD OF WARNING

There is one pitfall in the use of roses as a ground cover.

Don't ever use them near the property boundary.

If you have a slope from a public sidewalk up to your lawn, keep roses off it. If anyone should fall into them and be injured, you would be liable for damages. Children scuffling on their way home from school won't think of that—but you must!

Chapter 14

The "Minor" Types

The roses in the groups listed here are not minor in quality or charm—they just are not planted in such numbers as those in the previous groups.

HYBRID PERPETUALS

Just because these plants mark the "watershed" between the Old and Modern roses, they seem to be unjustly relegated to the former group in the public mind. This is unfortunate, as a goodly number are much like the better Hybrid Teas and are well worth growing. This is especially true where the climate is far from ideal, and also where tall, vigorous plants are needed in the background.

Just about all of the Hybrid Perpetuals have big blooms, the earlier ones somewhat flatter than is the current fashion, but the newer ones conform nicely—if that is an advantage. The more modern ones can match all but the best Hybrid Teas in the amount of bloom.

Hybrid Perpetuals need a different cultural pattern than the Hybrid Teas. They bloom in "waves" with little or no bloom in between. To reinforce the sheer mass of these recurrent blooming periods, you have to be lavish with the fertilizer and water in periods when a new "wave" is being developed. A safe rule of thumb is at least twice as much of each as you would use normally and maybe more of the water. Don't prune too hard, or the amount of bloom will be cut. The plants usually grow as upright shrubs to six feet. They are vigorous and generally quite hardy. Fragrance is usual, but not always present. Remember that not all Hybrid Perpetuals are old. Waldfree (Kordes 1960) is a lovely semidouble red, with golden stamens, fit for any garden.

PEGGING ROSES

A peculiar, but attractive and useful growing system was long used, especially for the stronger-growing Hybrid Perpetuals, although some long-caned shrubs and Pillar roses also used it. At present it is seldom used—a loss for all rose growers.

Briefly, the system consists of bending the canes sharply a few inches above the ground, and training them horizontally by tying them to pegs set firmly in the ground. The result? They produce far more blooms than with the natural upright growth pattern. Why? Without going into the physiological reasons, just about every bud on the cane develops on the horizontal canes. An upright cane retains many of the lower ones as "latent," so their potential blooms are never developed.

In this way, many normally upright shrubs can be used as ground covers or developed as stylized patterns. No usually planted ground-cover roses can match—in form, size, and generally numbers—Hybrid Perpetuals used in this way.

It must be confessed that there is extra work in this method, but that can be cut to a minimum if the bending and tying of the stems is done while the canes are young and still quite limber. If this is delayed too long, the canes become stiff and breakage is more or less inevitable. The change in direction should be quite abrupt, close to 90 degrees, for best results. Pegging can be used, with somewhat diminished results, for espaliers.

RECOMMENDATIONS

It is probable that gardeners will accept fewer of these cultivars than the more modern types—until they gain some real growing experience—at which time they could well look over the cultivars here listed.

AMERICAN BEAUTY

This is for nostalgia—except for the fragrance. The "live rose, shaded smoky carmine" (thanks, Dorothy), is distinctive on large, fully double, very fragrant blooms. They come repeatedly on a rather smallish (four-foot) plant. The climbing form is perhaps better, but I do not have it.

ARRILLAGA

For huge, light pink, beautifully formed blooms, which repeat moderately and are fragrant, try this one. This is a *big* plant, up to seven feet, and is pretty modern for the group, being introduced in 1929.

BARONNE PREVOST

The intensely double, flat flowers are typical of the best of the early Hybrid Perpetuals, and they have good fragrance. The color is pink, and the reverse of the petals has an opal tone. The bush is low, seldom growing more than four feet high.

BARONESS ROTHSCHILD

This is a magnificent rose, even if the fragrance is slight. The fully double blooms are large and cupped, with a clear pink color; she repeats well. The plant grows to about four feet. There is a white-flowered sport called White Baronesse.

FERDINAND PICHARD

Good striped roses are not too common, so you might like to try this one. The plants are vigorous, to six feet, and the cupped, double blooms are striped red and pink, or sometimes white; they are fragrant and repeat.

GENERAL JACQUEMINOT

This is the first rose I ever grew—at age ten—but I called it General Jack, as did almost everyone else. The fragrance of the large, velvety, deep crimson blooms was distinctive and generous—I can still recall it (50 years later!). The fall blooms are especially rich in color. The bush seldom grows more than five feet high, but is vigorous and hardy.

HENRY NEVARD

He is still popular and deserves to be, for the medium-sized blooms are rich crimson, very fragrant, and plentiful.

HUGH DICKSON

This is probably the tallest Hybrid Perpetual, growing to eight feet or more if given some support, and up to seven when grown as a shrub. The fragrant, repeating blooms are a clear, rich crimson.

Although Hybrid Perpetuals are seldom grown today,
there are a number that should be in every modern garden.
This is Paul Neyron, and his big, fragrant
pink blooms would grace any garden.

MRS. JOHN LAING

She is the most commonly seen pink, with big, fragrant flowers that repeat well. The big plants are vigorous and hardy.

PAUL NEYRON

If you like *big* blossoms, try this. They are fully double, slightly fragrant, and pink with a lilac undertone so distinctive that there is a color called Neyron Pink. The blooms repeat well on robust plants.

PRINCE CAMILLE DE ROHAN

Some gardeners are always looking for a *black* tulip, orchid, or whatever. In the roses you won't get any closer than this one. The medium-sized blooms are the deepest scarlet-maroon, and have an abundance of lovely scent. The plants do not have the usual vigor of the group, but they do produce a lot of blooms over a long period.

REINE DES VIOLETTES

Among the "blue" roses, one of the best is over a hundred years old—and equals or betters the modern ones. The true color is impossible to put into words, but is a mixture of pink and blue, with a touch of almost magenta. The blooms are very fragrant and repeat well. The plant is big, to seven feet or a bit more.

ROGER LAMBELIN

The wavy edges of the petals are white, but the remainder of the bloom is dark red. The double blooms have a bit of fragrance and appear regularly. Baron Girod de l'Ain is similar, but the white edge contrasts to a brighter red—and the latter is lower in growth, to about four feet. The Baron has more fragrance, and repeats well.

POLYANTHAS

It is difficult to determine just where this group merges into the Hybrid Polyanthas —and where *they* become Floribundas. No matter. These are among the best for bedding; that is, the plants are massed and produce sheets of bloom without any single identity. Bedding is more in the British tradition than American, but it is valuable from time to time. The better cultivars are dense and twiggy, and have innumerable little flowers of no special distinction of form, but good colors and constant bloom. They are quite hardy, especially the Poulsen originations; he bred for the rough climate of Denmark. Most of these grow no more than 18 inches high and can stand minimum spacings.

A SELECTION OF POLYANTHAS

CAMEO 7.5

This 40-year-old cultivar is seldom seen, but it is very useful, and nice, where a *low* bedding plant is needed, as it grows no more than 15 inches high. The plentiful blooms are borne in clusters, and are an appealing salmon-pink.

CECILE BRUNNER 7.7

This is grown, to a great extent, for the perfectly formed, light pink buds to be worn in a corsage or as a boutonniere. The climbing form is delightful as a garden plant.

GLORIA MUNDI 6.5

Quite vigorous to 20 inches, this is a very prolific bedder with pompons of red-orange in large clusters.

MARGO(T) KOSTER 7.7

A compact, low plant covered with larger, salmon-orange blooms all season long. Second only to The Fairy.

PERLE D'OR 7.7

A "sweetheart type" with perfect, peach-pink blooms on a low plant. For boutonniere or corsage use, as a contrast for Cecile Brunner.

POULSEN'S BEDDER 7.4

Similar to Margo Koster, but the freely produced blooms are a clear rose-pink. The growth habit is fairly dense and neat.

THE FAIRY 8.5

This doesn't really belong here, but it is closer than placing her with the Floribundas, as some do. Big mounds of sprawling canes bear a *continuous* supply of light pink, small blooms in clusters. Essentially disease free, this rose grows beautifully—in good soil and in that which is less than good—even in some shade. Give ample room, four feet or more. This is a must for every garden—rose or otherwise!

MINIATURES

These smallest of all roses have, to use a *true* cliché, an elfin charm. The canes are tiny, as are the leaves and flowers. Yet they hold all the grace and charm of their larger sisters. The extremely tiny—mostly older—cultivars run from six to eight inches in height with half-inch blooms. These are mostly for the hobbyist, the alpine gardener, or for the maker of miniature gardens. The newer cultivars, however, may be expected to reach about a foot, and the beautifully formed flowers will be somewhat larger. Reds, pinks, whites, and yellows are to be found. These are beautiful as edging plants, or in gardens scaled to their size. As pot plants they are unexcelled. Bloom in the better cultivars is constant.

Recently a new dimension has been added—Climbing Miniatures, which grow from two and a half to five feet high. Pink Cameo was the first, and is still one of the best. All of their parts are in scale, making a most dainty and lovely picture.

Among the older cultivars there are several that are still grown, including *R. rouletti* (the first, 1912), pink; Oakingham Ruby and Tom Thumb, both red, and Baby Gold Star, yellow.

Among the newer kinds, especially good for growing outdoors as edgings for borders, are:

Reds: Little Buckeroo, Dian, Nova Red, Tiny Jack.

Pinks: June Time, Eleanor, Baby Ophelia, Tiny Jill.

Whites: Frosty, Cinderella, Easter Morning.

Blends: Jeanie Williams, Baby Darling.

Yellow: Yellow Doll.

Climbers: Pink Cameo, Climbing Jackie, Candy Cane.

Ralph Moore (Sequoia Nurseries), dean of American breeders of Miniature roses, has recently made an outstanding breakthrough in producing Mossed Miniatures. The first was Fairy Moss, with but little moss on its light pink blooms. The next generation brought heavy moss on Kara, with its small, red buds that open as single, medium pink blooms. The plant is bushy and ten inches high.

TREE ROSES

The usual Tree roses are Hybrid Teas or Floribundas budded high on an upright stem, forming a head which produces the blooms. Two unusual, and worthwhile,

Tree roses make fine accent plants.
This planting, however, is rather stark.
It would be tremendously improved by underplanting
with some bushy Floribundas.

kinds are not often seen, but are well worth growing: Tree Climbing Floribundas (such as Summer Snow), which make a weeping head, and Climbing Miniatures. Another novelty is to have two to four cultivars budded to a single stem—which is a bit flashy for some of us. With all Tree roses order early, as the supply seldom equals the demand; this is especially true of the Miniatures.

The making of Tree roses is complicated and long drawn out; they are therefore expensive. Except in mild climates—as described in Chapter 8—they take a lot of work. But where the climate is kind and the proper rootstock is used, they could well be used more often—they give an accent to beds of bush roses and other landscape features that nothing else can.

The rootstocks IXL or multiflora can be grown to a single, staked stem until it reaches the proper height and thickness. Then the desired cultivar is budded, two to four buds for a balanced head. The usual heights are three or four feet, but some six-footers are produced in Hybrid Teas and Floribundas. In any event, all Tree roses should be staked if there is any chance that they may be exposed to even fairly stiff winds.

For severe climates, where Tree roses are a liability, the best solution is to bud a rootstock of multiflora with a rugosa stem and that with the desired cultivar.

Not a great number of cultivars are generally offered, as those with very stout canes produce an awkward head; light, graceful canes shape up much better.

A new stock (at least to me) has recently been added—De la Grifferaie, by Jackson and Perkins. It is said to be very hardy and strong, and it is also supposed to bend well for winter protection. I look forward to growing a few trees budded on this.

Most of the Tree Miniatures are either 12 or 18 inches high.

Chapter 15

The Species and Shrub Roses

It is unfortunate that most rose growers limit their choice of plants to one or more of the groups already discussed, neglecting the species, Shrub, and Old roses. They surely limit the landscape effects possible, and they just as surely limit their pleasure.

In these three groups you can find delightful plants for edgings, hedges, waterside gardens, espaliers, seaside plantings, ground covers, and mixed borders. There are more entirely self-reliant plants in these three groups than in all the other roses combined—a fact to be weighed in this day of less and less qualified help.

THE SPECIES

The species, like any other group, are a mixed lot. There are the fine ones, such as *R. rugosa* and *R. moyesii* or even *R. palustris*. Then there is the Macartney rose, *R. bracteata*, which is a devilish weed where it is hardy—it can take over hundreds of acres of crop and pasture land, being impervious to anything except dynamite, a

Old plants of the China roses are still to be found around old homes
and even cellar holes—where the buildings have long disappeared.
They are extremely hardy and require next to no care.
The large, fully double flowers are pink and sweetly fragrant.

bulldozer, or floods of very strong weed killers. *R. multiflora*, at one time widely advertised by some unscrupulous merchandisers as a fine hedge plant, even for suburban properties, is only somewhat less of a pest. Both of these have produced good hybrids—but leave the species alone!

THE BETTER SPECIES AND SHRUBS

Rosa blanda is the fulfillment of a dream for those in the most extreme climates— its natural range goes to Hudson Bay! The single, pink blooms are followed by large crimson hips, carried on almost thornless canes up to five feet.

The "wild rose" of the East is *R. carolina*, with its single, fragrant pink flowers showing for weeks, starting in June. This you will have to collect in the wild—so be selective. Some grow only three feet high, some few to five feet. The size of the flower also varies, from two to three inches. This makes a good, low-maintenance hedge plant, as it spreads by suckers and soon makes an impenetrable barrier.

Some nurseries play up the "green rose," *R. chinensis viridifolia*, as something special. Don't bother—it's an oddity, not a pretty thing.

The fame of the sweetbrier, *R. eglanteria*, started early in the South and has spread widely since. Unlike most plants, its fragrance—the fragrance of apples— comes from the leaves, not the small single flowers; it becomes more intense when wet. Why most of these are grown in the South is a mystery, as they will develop, in time, to eight feet or more even in quite cold climates.

Somewhere in the shrub or mixed border—away from other roses—every gardener should have at least one Austrian Copper rose, *R. foetida bicolor*. The isolation from other roses stems from the great susceptibility to black spot—making it the "Typhoid Mary" of the rose garden. But the vigorous, six-foot plant bears incredibly brilliant single flowers. The inside of the petals is bright orange-scarlet, and the reverse is deep gold. The habit is dense and twiggy and the leaves are very small, giving a ferny look. The species, *R. foetida*, has yellow flowers, and it is worth growing even if it is never as spectacular as Austrian Copper. The Persian Yellow rose, *R. foetida persiana*, has double yellow flowers on a bush that is much less temperamental than most other yellow species. It is interesting to note that this has never been found in the wild.

Another natural hybrid with lovely, fragrant, double yellow flowers is Harison's Yellow, *R. harisoni*. It comes from the Scotch rose, so it is very spiny. The vigorous, six-foot plant, a very hardy one, usually blooms but once, but Dorothy Stemler (Tillotson's Roses) says that by withholding water and fertilizer during the summer you can coax some autumn bloom. The leaves are quite tiny, and the hips are black and small.

Still another good yellow is *R. hugonis*, with its four- to six-foot canes almost bare of thorns. The foliage is fernlike. The single flowers appear in May, and they are followed by black hips. The graceful arching canes are iron-hardy.

Getting away from all the above yellows leads us (alphabetically) to one of the most striking of all roses—species or hybrid—*R. moyesii*. This grows to ten feet, not always as gracefully as you would wish, but it is covered with single flowers that range from terra-cotta to ruby-red—a dazzling display that has to be seen to be believed. The foliage is a bluish green, and there are from 7 to 13 leaflets, giving an airy feeling to the plant. The hips are "pitcher shaped," of fair size, and are bright orange-red; they make almost as dazzling a display as the flowers do. The English would call this a "miffy" plant—it can sulk or thrive for no discernible reason. If you can please it, however, it is a joy.

Some of the hybrid offspring of *R. moyesii* are less temperamental than their parent—yet they have her charm. Geranium Red (not the Floribunda of the same name) has two-inch scarlet blooms. Nevada has large four-inch blooms that are white or flesh-colored, sometimes with a bit of red flecking. The plant is more graceful, with arching canes to five or six feet. This one has repeat bloom—a big plus.

Where a low-growing, easy-to-care-for plant is needed, *R. nitida* could well be the answer. It grows only 18 inches to 2 feet tall, and has single, bright pink blooms. The stems are crimson, and are covered with red hairs; the thorns are red, too, and the leaves turn red in the fall. The round hips are red as well. This one makes a fine, low hedge plant.

The awesome name *R. omeiensis pteracantha* is redeemed by a most distinctive plant. The small white flowers are unique among roses, for they have but four petals. The dense plant grows to ten feet. But the most striking point (pun intended) lies in the large, translucent red thorns, so elongated that they almost meet each other along the stem. Try to plant this on the western side of the garden so that it can be viewed against the setting sun. Some nurseries list this as *R. sericia pteracantha*, which is incorrect. I haven't been able to locate a source in this country for either Hidcote Gold or Red Wing, so someone should import them. Both have yellow flowers, and the latter has large, winged thorns that hold their "beautiful translucent red color throughout the winter."

One of the few roses that will grow well in damp ground is the Swamp rose, *R. palustris.* This makes a big, vigorous plant in moist locations, up to six or even eight feet. In dry locations it will seldom go more than two feet. It bears bright pink flowers in June, with some little repeating in late summer and fall. This and *R.*

nitida are not produced commercially in this country, so you must either collect them in the wild yourself or buy collected plants.

The Tien Shan, or Incense, rose, *R. primula*, has lovely early, single, yellow flowers on short stems coming from the very prickly seven-foot canes. The red hips which follow, unfortunately, are shed early. The foliage is fragrant, the more so when wet. Tuck a few dried leaves in the drawer with your handkerchiefs and gloves and a few more in your purse. It's a nice change from lavender, or (in the drawer) a potpourri.

A rose of many names is *R. roxburghii*. It is called the burr, chestnut, and chinquapin rose in those areas of the South where it is hardy. The large, flat, double flowers are deep rose-pink in the center, fading to a medium pink at the edge of the petals; it repeats. The height varies enormously, from four to ten feet. The name comes from the prickles on the hips—arrangers love them. The only thorns are a pair of bright red, upward-curving ones at the base of each leaf-stalk; the leaves have quite small leaflets, 9 to 15 per leaf. The variety *R. r. rubra* has, naturally, red flowers, and the modern cultivar Cinnabar (Tantau, 1945) has clusters of semi-double vermilion blooms, which repeat.

Another rose grown for its foliage, as well as the recurrent pink flowers, is *R. rubrifolia*. The leaves are rosy-green all season long, until they turn red in the fall. The canes and hips are red, too, on hardy plants about five feet high. This one deserves a wider acceptance, for it is just about trouble free, and most attractive.

ROSA RUGOSA AND ITS HYBRIDS

High on any list of the best roses there has to be a place for the Rugosas. They are very hardy and trouble free; have a good dense habit of growth; are usually five or

One of the loveliest of all white roses is Blanc Double de Coubert,
a Hybrid Rugosa. The semidouble flowers are followed
by lacquer-red hips, which contrast beautifully
with the wrinkled foliage.

six feet high; are well clothed with rich, deep green, wrinkled, and disease-free foliage, which turns orange or red in the fall. They repeat their fragrant bloom, and from midsummer on bear both blooms and big, bulbous, red hips, so glossy they look as if they had been lacquered.

Every gardener near the sea knows the Rugosas, as they can stand salt spray, gale winds, and will even grow in almost pure sand. On the shore north of Boston, I once found several eight-inch twigs of a Rugosa peeping out of the top of a sand dune—bearing both flowers and brilliant hips. On digging down, I discovered six feet of stem before I found any roots!

Rosa rugosa bears satiny, single, magenta-pink flowers, while *R. r. alba* is the purest white. These contrast strongly with the massed golden stamens. *R. r rosea* sounds nice, but I have never seen it.

Suggested Rugosa Cultivars ...

It is difficult to select just a few of the better cultivars, but here are some I regard highly.

Agnes 7.4

She grows six feet high and bears very fragrant, rich yellow flowers.

Belle Poitevine 7.9

The double, fragrant, lilac-pink blooms appear repeatedly on a plant six or more feet high.

Blanc Double de Coubert 7.7

The semidouble, fragrant white blooms are borne on plants five to seven feet high. The bloom falls off about the first of September.

CONRAD FERDINAND MEYER 7.0

A neighbor of mine grows this as a Climber, in a tree. It is usually described as growing to eight feet, but with support it will go over ten. The large, double, light pink flowers are quite fragrant.

FRAU DAGMAR HASTRUP 8.0

The flowers are single, pink, and have a delicate satiny texture; the fragrance is good.

F. J. GROOTENDORST 7.5

The small flowers are fringed and borne in clusters, and are bright red. They look more like garden pinks than roses. Pink Grootendorst and Grootendorst Supreme, crimson, have the same type of bloom, which I sometimes think is more novel than beautiful. They all grow about six feet high.

MAX GRAF 8.1

(This has been treated under ground covers, page 152).

MRS. ANTHONY WATERER 7.7

The intensely fragrant, deep crimson blooms are borne on a less vigorous plant, which grows only three to four feet high.

NOVA ZEMBLA 8.3

This is like C. F. Meyer, except that the color is white.

ROSE À PARFUM DE L'HAY 7.6

What a name! There will ever be disagreement as to which rose is the most fragrant. My friend Dick Thomson says Crimson Glory, and I admire his taste. But this one

Frau Dagmar Hastrup (what a name to Western ears!)
is a modern Hybrid Rugosa, with unbelievably graceful blooms,
which are followed by huge, colorful hips.
These make wonderful conserves, rich in vitamin C.

is, for me, the *ne plus ultra*. The double carmine flowers are borne only in June and July, on big six-foot plants. No matter, the pleasure of knowing that fragrance will stay with you the year round!

SARAH VAN FLEET 8.3
She is still popular for her fragrant, rose-red blooms produced over a long period. The height is usually around eight feet.

SIR THOMAS LIPTON 7.0
A worthy tribute to a fine gentleman, this husky, six-foot plant has plenty of double white blooms.

. . . AND SOME OPEN-POLLENATED CROSSES
The great rose hybridizer Wilhelm Kordes used Max Graf as the seed parent of several open-pollenated crosses. The resulting plants have been named *R. kordesii*, and some lovely things are in the group. Not all of them are available here, but you might try these, which are.

DORTMUND 8.3
The single, bright crimson blooms have a white "eye," and they are produced all season long. The plant will go to 14 feet or so when used as a Climber, or to about ten when "pegged." The heavy, glossy leaves seem to laugh at disease, and the plant is very hardy.

ELMSHORN 7.7
Large trusses of small carmine-red blooms appear "from June to November." The plant is five feet high.

HAMBURG 7.3

The semidouble crimson blooms are borne in clusters all season. The upright plant will reach six feet.

HEIDELBURG

The "fairly double," sparkling flowers have been called "a flame shot mixture of crimson and scarlet." They are carried on long stems on a five-foot plant.

KASSEL

When grown on a wall or trellis, this plant will grow to more than 12 feet, but 8 feet is tops as a free-standing shrub. The deep crimson, double flowers are borne in clusters. It repeats well. A real beauty!

LEVERKUSEN

This is much like a slightly less vigorous Dortmund, as far as plant and foliage are concerned. The flowers are fully double, high-centered, and fragrant, and they glow with a soft yellow color.

MAIGOLD 8.0

This is another yellow, but a rich yellow with bronzy tones. The flowers are fragrant and are borne in great clusters all season. Grown as a shrub it will reach eight feet; with support, somewhat higher.

The large hips of all the Rugosas are universally admired for their shape and color, but they have another good point—they make fine conserves, which are especially rich in vitamin C. It was from these hips, collected by the ton from the hedgerows of England, that the British obtained this needed vitamin when World War II cut off the import of citrus fruits.

*The Musk roses are noted not only for their beauty but for their rich,
long-lasting fragrance. This is Buff Beauty, which has yellow buds,
stained apricot. They open to rich gold
and fade to a creamy shade. It will grow in light shade.*

The Scotch or Burnet rose, *R. spinosissima*, is sometimes grown in gardens where a very tough, hardy plant is needed. It grows to five feet, with light canes seemingly covered with thorns. The single, cream-colored flowers appear early and persist into early summer. The hips are small and black, with no ornamental value. Like the Rugosas, the Scotch rose will stand the savage winds, the salt spray, and excessively sandy soils of the seashore. On the whole, however, this plant is more valuable as the parent of better things, even though it is a nightmare for plant breeders.

Much better is a botanical variety from Siberia, *R. s. altaica*. This is more graceful in habit, and bears large, creamy-yellow flowers. *R. s. andrewsii* is the best of the pinks.

For a century and a half Stanwell Perpetual has been a favorite of many gardeners. It repeats well with its sweetly fragrant, blush-white blooms. The plants are graceful, growing from four to six feet high, with a grayish-green foliage.

In recent times breeders have taken to the difficult task of breeding Scotch roses. Herr Kordes has been eminently successful in producing some of the loveliest shrubs available. The "Spring Series" certainly proves this. Frühlingsgold grows to seven feet, with graceful, arching canes bearing large, semidouble, fragrant flowers of a pure golden color. Frühlingsmorgan is a magnificent single, with the center soft yellow and the petal edges a cherry-pink; the stamens are maroon. The fragrance of both is fantastic in quantity and quality. Karl Forster is a magnificent shrub that blooms all summer long, while the two above last for two weeks or so in late May. The blooms are semidouble and pure white; the usual height is about five feet.

In this country Roy Shepherd, the eminent rose historian, crossed *R. spinosissima* with Soeur Thérèse and produced Golden Wings. This four-foot shrub can take temperatures down to 0 degrees F. without protection. The single, fragrant, sulfur-yellow flowers have a ring of reddish-bronze stamens and repeat until frost. Like many other Shrubs, this one needs next to no pruning for the first two or three years, so it can develop its real shape and blooming habit.

A large number of other fine Shrub roses are more often considered Old roses; they will be discussed in the next chapter.

Chapter 16

Roses from Grandmother's Garden

Many rose growers, especially novices and exhibitors, ask, "Why bother with Old roses when the new ones are so great?" They cite the high-pointed buds and "exhibition type" blooms, improved disease resistance on better foliage, more vigor, and the wide range of colors in the newer cultivars. Their battle cry is "What's new?"

They have their points—these are the criteria of the times.

But fashions change, sometimes going full circle. Witness women's—and even men's—clothes. Because you enjoy today's roses you don't have to limit yourself to them alone. If you do, you needlessly limit your enjoyment.

Those gardeners who are not slaves to the fashion of the moment can enjoy the flat, the cupped, and even the quartered blooms of another day. They can have beautiful colors not known in Modern roses. They can revel in the ease of growing some of the earliest kinds—such as the Gallicas, Damasks, and Centifolias—even in severe climates. And, of course, many of the old fragrances are unique. In other words, those whose taste is so developed that they can ignore fashion will probably grow some Old roses—and widen their enjoyment immeasurably!

THE BEGINNINGS

Strictly speaking, we can choose any rose from the "presently known" beginnings—that is, China during the Chin-Nung (Shen-Nung) Dynasty (c. 2737–2697 B.C.) or the Tigris-Euphrates Valley during the reign of King Sargon I of Ur (c. 2637–2582 B.C.). But we don't know which roses were grown this early—and although by 200 B.C. the Chinese had a number of different kinds in their gardens, and a special method of culture for them, we have no record of what these were, either.

The first specific rose we can pin down is the Autumn Damask, *Rosa gallica bifera*, growing on the island of Samor during the tenth century B.C. It was described as "flowering twice a year and being used in the cult of Aphrodite."

It wasn't until Theophrastus (c. 300 B.C.) that the different roses were described. But, as the Greeks were rather indifferent gardeners, it is probable that he merely cataloged the wild roses that were known.

The Romans were much better gardeners than the Greeks, and they grew huge fields of roses to supply blooms for banquets and festivals. How many kinds they grew is not known, but again the Autumn Damask turned up in the famous plantings at Paestum. The Romans even carried roses to the lands they conquered.

With the fall of Rome, monks tending monastery gardens saved many kinds—more, probably, for medicine, seasoning, and cosmetics than for beauty.

As travel became safer during the Renaissance, traders, diplomats, and scholars began to exchange plants, including roses. Those of the Near East did much to broaden the horizons of European gardeners. The herbalist Gerard, in England, listed 14 kinds in 1597 and, only 32 years later, Parkinson listed 24.

Almost everything up to this point that is available and desirable has been described in the preceding chapter.

THE FRENCH ROSES

The French rose, *Rosa gallica*, is red, extremely fragrant, and vigorous. Because it was thought to cure quite a number of diseases, it was found in just about every monastery and castle garden. As it spreads by suckers and also sets good crops of seeds and is very hardy, it soon grew all over the lands that had been part of the Roman Empire. It probably arrived in England around A.D. 1100 and became known as "ye badge of England"—and later as the Red Rose of Lancaster. It is seldom grown today.

Much better known today is the Apothecary rose, *R. gallica officinalis*, in Europe called the "Provins rose," which came early to this country. It is still to be found in old gardens, by deserted cellar holes, and along the roadsides. The petals hold their rich fragrance extraordinarily well on drying. Because of this, great fields were planted to this rose near Provins, where the petals were made into medicines, perfumes, and confections. It is semidouble and deep red.

Rosa gallica versicolor has been called Rosa Mundi and Rosamonde. It has also been called the "best of all striped roses." Named after Rosamonde (Clifford), the "Fair Rosamonde," mistress of Henry II of England, this sport of the Apothecary rose has white petals that bear a motley of stripes and flecks ranging from pink through crimson to almost purple.

Unfortunately, the Normandy rose, *R. g. phoenicia*, doesn't seem to be commercially available—but it is worth a search, even if that means importing it. The tallest

In Provins, France, a main industry is growing the Apothecary rose,
Rosa gallica officinalis, *to distill its intense fragrance for perfume making.*
The bright red, semidouble blooms have a center
set with golden yellow stamens. It is hardy and easy to grow.

Gallica, it grows six feet high and wider than that. It has glossy leaves and bears fat, globular flowers (much like the Cabbage roses), which are brilliant crimson. Another contrary feature lies in the many thorns—many more than most Gallicas.

Among the more frequently grown Gallicas are those below.

SUGGESTED GALLICAS

ALAIN BLANCHARD

Here is a rose with (in the true sense) unique color. The single, rather cup-shaped, crimson blooms have irregular patches of purple, all set off by the bright gold of the stamens. The canes are thorny. The sport of this, Panachee, with stripes, not blotches, is not to be confused with Perle des Panachées, which is a lovely, semi-double white with flecks and stripes of crimson, contrasting prettily with the yellow stamens.

BELLE DE CRECY

The flat, double flowers are borne on four-foot plants, and the violet-pink color has a "silvery-bluish" shading. As the bloom ages, blue-violet takes over. Very fragrant.

CAMAIEUX

Although the plant is low-growing (26 to 28 inches), the white stripes on the almost maroon blooms are delightful, even when they turn dark as the cup-shaped blooms fade.

CARDINAL RICHELIEU

Big, to five or even six feet, and wide, this rose is as dramatic as Cardinal Richelieu himself. The canes are almost thornless, and the glossy leaves are bright green. The big, bulbous blooms are a rich, wine-red, infused with violet and overlaid with a velvety sheen. This is a must!

GEORGE VIBERT

The flat blooms are usually quartered, and the petals reflex as the bloom opens. The petals have alternate stripes of pink and deep carmine.

MARCEL BOURGOUIN

One of the better low-growing kinds, he grows only 30 inches high. The purple-maroon color of the almost flat blooms brilliantly accents the golden stamens.

TUSCANY SUPERB

The almost thornless canes grow to four feet. The plant blooms but once, the blooms being blackish-maroon with the sheen of velvet. The fragrant flowers are flat, and the golden stamens contrast strongly with the many dark petals.

THE CABBAGE ROSES

You may know the Cabbage roses as Provence roses, "roses of a hundred leaves," or even as "rose de la peintures." Although they are not of great importance in the gardens of today, they played a big part in the development of the Hybrid Perpetuals, and even the Hybrid Teas.

The plants are rather lax in habit, and grow from three to about six feet high; the taller ones sometimes need support. The thorns are small, and the rather dull leaves are decidedly rounded. The blooming period covers several weeks in June and July. They will tolerate poor soils better than most roses. Don't prune them hard—just cut back the longest canes, remove dead or damaged wood, and then thin the center a bit. Few, if any, roses are hardier.

There is no garden that could not be improved by adding
a piece or two of good sculpture. While this Saint Francis is almost trite,
it is saved by being beautifully done and "makes"
the garden picture. The rose is City of York.

Two of the names given to *R. centifolia* come directly from the flowers. There are a hundred petals or more, and these petals overlap, as in a cabbage. It grows five feet high, and the typical globular blooms are rose-pink and large. The color range of the group runs from the faintest blush to a deep rose-pink, but never red.

A Few to Try

ROSA CENTIFOLIA BULLATA

The globular, light pink blooms shade to a richer pink in the center. The jade-green leaves are very large, and they take on bronze and red tones in the fall. The fragrance is strong—for a Cabbage. Under good conditions the bush will reach six feet.

DE MEAUX

This much smaller bush, to three feet, is covered with very small (half inch), double, clear pink flowers. Their airy grace and long-lasting quality make them a natural for cutting.

RED PROVENCE

The large, cupped blooms are deep carmine-rose and very fragrant. The plant is moderately vigorous.

TOUR DE MALAKOFF

The very large, fragrant blooms have been described as "peonylike," and they have a bewildering color pattern. Veins and splashes of violet and lilac overlay the basic crimson-red until, on fading, the blooms turn a softer color, almost like gray smoke. The plants are vigorous to six feet. They should have some support, during blooming time at least, as the limber canes can't hold the weight of the many large blooms.

VIERGE DE CLERY

Other names for this include White Provence and Unique Blanche. The buds show some pink, but the many fragrant blooms open white. This cultivar is very useful, as it starts blooming late and lasts longer than most. The plant will grow from four to a bit more than five feet.

THE MOSS ROSES

A true Moss rose has sepals that envelop the bud, and these have hairs that have been transformed into *soft*, mosslike growths. The amount of moss varies and usually extends down the pedicel (top of the stem); in some cases it even shows on the leaves as well. Generally the moss is green, but some is red. All of these are mutations of Cabbage roses.

On the other hand, some Damasks have mutations involving sepals that are more or less thickly set with prickles. These sepals usually do not fully enclose the bud. To the purists these are not true Moss roses—but some catalog writers and gardeners squeeze them into the group, regardless.

The Common Moss, *R. centifolia muscosa*, is typical of the group. It grows from four to six feet high, has fairly large, double, cupped, very fragrant blooms. Here the flowers are pink and come fairly late—once only. There is a white form as well.

SUGGESTIONS

BLANCHE MOREAU

Even if this is a "Damask Moss," it is very good, with bristly, reddish moss. Under good conditions this will give some fall bloom, for the Damask Rose de Quatre

The "true" Moss roses carry the soft "moss"
not only on the buds but on the pedicels as well.
This is Gloire des Mousseux,
one of the loveliest of them all.

Saisons is in its breeding. The plant is vigorous, and the small blooms are pure white.

COMTESSE DE MURINAIS

The pink-tinted buds open pure white on vigorous plants, which will reach six feet. The fragrance is wonderful. She blooms heavily, if only once. The blue-green leaves have a bronzy tone.

CRESTED MOSS

This is perhaps better known as Chapeau de Napoléon. The sepals have thick, "tufted" moss. The flowers are pink and very fragrant. Although it is once-blooming, that "once" lasts for weeks. The plants are not as tall as most, with four feet or a bit more being usual.

DEUIL DE PAUL FONTAINE

This rose is different from other Mosses, for his breeding is very complex. The plant grows to three or four feet, with reddish and very thorny canes and reddish leaves. The big, fully double flowers are well quartered but not very fragrant. You will have to see the flowers to know what they are like. The closest I can come to describing them is that the blackish-crimson petals are splashed with reddish-brown and purple. He repeats in the fall. Unique is the word.

GABRIEL NOYELLE

Actually, this gal is an imposter here—for she was introduced as late as 1933. But she is a good Moss and also repeats. She is vigorous to six feet. The buds open pinky-salmon, then shift to deep cream as the semidouble, fragrant blooms open fully.

GLOIRE DE MOUSSEUX

This one has "more moss than anybody"! The sepals are considerably longer than the buds, giving a "fringed" effect. The pink flowers have deeper tones in the middle; they are very large and fragrant. A well-grown plant can reach five feet.

JEANNE DE MONTFORD

This is the tallest Moss I have ever seen—a full eight feet! It can be used as a Pillar or Climber. The blooms are not as large as some, but are a nice shell pink, which fades to light blush around the yellow stamens; the fragrance is refreshing.

MADAME LOUIS LEVEQUE

Quite a few discerning growers consider this the finest of all Moss roses. The large, well-quartered blooms are intensely fragrant and they repeat. The distinctive color is a blend of lilac and pink. The plant grows to five or even six feet.

MARIE DE BLOIS

The deep rose flowers are remarkable because, although they are quite double when fully open, they show golden stamens within the central petals, which are most gracefully frilled. The strong fragrance is spicy. A height of about five feet is usual.

MOUSSELINE (ALFRED DE DALMES)

This compact plant is unusual in two ways. It seldom gets over two feet high, and it blooms repeatedly all season long. The small, light pink flowers are only slightly fragrant. It makes a wonderful edging or low hedge plant.

Sculpture in the garden does not need to be big and overbearing.
Here two small doves and a tiny pool
enhance the beauty of Betty Prior. Note also the hanging pots
on the split-cedar background fence.

SALAT

The double, rich-pink blooms have the fragrance of musk and repeat "almost like a Floribunda," but the plant is twice as high. The moss comes from the Damask side of its breeding, so it is rather stiff.

STRIPED MOSS

The color of the flat, very double flowers varies with the weather. Usually they are bright crimson and white, but on occasion they can be rich or pale pink. It blooms but once. The moss, thorns, and canes are red, and the leaves have red edges. Usually four to five feet.

THE DAMASKS

There are two main groups within this major group. The Summer Damasks come from *R. damascena* and bloom but once. The Autumn Damasks come from *R. d. bifera* and bloom in summer and autumn and sometimes in between.

The former group is more vigorous and upright, although more arching in habit than the Gallicas. The leaves are decidedly grayish, and the blooms are all double to some degree. This group should be pruned at the end of flowering, rather than in late winter.

The Autumn Damasks are generally slightly smaller and the canes more supple, so that growing them on a wall or other support is often resorted to, even though they can be grown freestanding. The leaves are a slightly yellowish green, with no gray tones. Here, pruning should be done in spring, only removing dead, damaged, too crowded, or too long growth.

The color range is similar in both groups, varying shades of pink or white, and the fragrance is of the same quality, but the Autumn Damasks have more of it. They are about the only kind grown in the Balkans and Near East for the production of attar of roses.

A BEGINNING SELECTION

CELSIANA 8.0

One of the most popular kinds, this one has small clusters (three to five) of large, flat blooms. They are blush pink with golden stamens in the middle; the fragrance is wonderful. The leaves are gray-green on both sides. The arching canes grow to five feet.

MADAME HARDY 9.1

The five-foot plants have a richer green color because of the mixed parentage. The clustered blooms are clear white and cup-shaped. When fully open there is a green "eye" in the center. This is an old-time favorite, and should remain so. Richard Thomson claims it has a fragrance more normal to the Albas, but I can't vouch for that—it just has a lovely fragrance.

MARIE LOUISE 7.7

The huge blooms of pale pink have a green "eye" when fully opened, but the pedicels can't support the weight if the weather is wet. When the canes are given the support of a trellis or are espaliered, however, the effect is in no way marred. The many-petaled, flat blooms have an intense fragrance. The rich green leaves are attractive. She blooms but once.

ROSA DAMASCENA BIFERA

The oldest of all is *R. d. bifera*, the Autumn Damask, which has been grown since at least 2000 B.C. The fully double blooms show a definite quartering. Several of the pink blooms are borne together, and they are very fragrant. The leaves are a rather yellowish green. The repeating bloom is a big asset.

ROSE DU ROI 8.3

This color is beyond the usual pattern for the group. It changes from the bright red of the center to a deep blackish-red at the outer petals, with somewhat lighter tones on the reverse side. The blooms are of medium size, and have a heavy, true Damask fragrance. The plants will reach three feet or a bit more. Rose de Rescht is so similar that there is little reason to grow both.

THE ALBAS

This group has a few very fine members, but on the whole has more historic than garden value. *R. alba semiplena* is the symbol of the House of York. All of the early kinds were white, but later introductions "progressed" to clear pink.

The species grows to five feet, but the cultivars are usually taller. The flowers are produced but once, but the hips are large, "pitcher shaped," and attractive. The fragrance is distinctive, and has been likened to the heavy fragrance of hyacinths.

A FEW SUGGESTIONS

FELICITY PARMENTIER

She blooms in clusters, and as the soft pink flowers open past the cupped shape, the petals fold back until the flowers form a ball, showing a green "eye." These have the distinctive fragrance. The vigorous plant grows to five feet, and has typically grayish-green foliage.

KOËNIGIN VON DANEMARCK

The bush is more open than most Albas, and peaks near five feet. The large, very double, rose-pink blooms, which are fragrant, are models of quartered blooms.

MAIDEN'S BLUSH

This is the most popular of all Albas, a "pretty conceit" in itself, but the French are more direct in calling it Cuisse de Nymph Emue ("thigh of a passionate nymph"). I can't vouch for the comparison, but the bud has a flesh-tone pink before opening and fades to white. As with all Albas, the fragrance is lovely. The bush will reach six feet or more; it is clothed with rough, gray-green leaves, which are essentially pest free.

THE MUSK ROSES

This is a very diverse group, ranging from four-foot shrubs to Climbers 40 or more feet tall. Some bloom but once and others are in constant bloom.

Rosa moschata is only for large gardens, for it grows to 25 feet. The variety *R. m. brunoni* is even larger. The single, clustered white flowers appear but once, but the bright orange hips light up the plant in late summer and fall. Probably the best way to use this plant is to give it a tree to clamber over.

The Hybrid Musks, unlike all the other groups in this chapter, belong to this century—and new ones are still appearing from time to time. You may quibble at their being listed here, but they really don't fit anywhere else. In fact, why they are listed as Musks at all is a pertinent question, as they resulted from a cross between *R. multiflora* and the Noisette Rêve d'Or (which had *R. moschata* in its ancestry).

Regardless of how they are classified, there are a number of Hybrid Musks that are well worth growing today—some as shrubs, but most as Pillars or Climbers.

All of them bloom in trusses, repeatedly, and most are fragrant. Many have attractive hips in the fall. The vigorous growth ranges from 3 to 12 feet. The plants are very easy to care for, as they are quite disease resistant; they are more shade tolerant than most roses.

SUGGESTIONS

In the following listing, no attempt will be made to separate the old from the new — they range from just after World War I to the present.

BELINDA 7.8

Although she is vigorous, she grows to only five feet. The one-inch, semidouble, fragrant, clear pink flowers are borne in large clusters. Easy and lovely.

BUFF BEAUTY 7.7

The fully double, three-inch blooms come from buds that are salmon tinged with yellow and creamy gold.

CORNELIA 7.9

Grow this as a Climber reaching up to ten feet. The small flowers will appear in big trusses. In summer the buds are orange tinged with red, and the open flowers are a soft blend of pink and yellow. With the coolness of fall these colors deepen.

KATHLEEN 7.7

The single, light pink flowers are borne in big clusters. Everyone remarks on the similarity to apple blossoms. The fragrance has the true "musk" scent. The plants are big, to ten or twelve feet, and need support.

The graceful arching canes of Nevada,
liberally sprinkled with the almost single,
creamy-white flowers,
make it one of the best of all Shrub roses.

LAVENDER LASSIE

This is bragging a bit, for the color is more nearly a lilac-pink. The large, fully double, fragrant flowers are produced all season long. Vigorous to ten feet or more.

NASTARANA 8.4

This is the smallest of the Musks at around three feet. The clustered, rather small, semidouble, fragrant blooms open white from soft pink buds—all season long.

PAX 7.2

Few white Climbers in *any* class can match Pax in the loveliness and number of blooms or in the length of the blooming season. The creamy, fragrant blooms are big—up to five inches—and although they are semidouble the first impression is that they are really double. The long, slender canes will make a graceful shrub to about seven feet or a Climber to ten. Penelope is much the same, but has more or less pink in the somewhat smaller blooms.

WILHELM AND WILL SCARLET 7.5

Which of these is the best red of the group is a tossup. The first is a double, deep red, which is fragrant and repeats. Will Scarlet is semidouble, a bright scarlet that repeats constantly—even when it carries the clusters of orange hips from the first blooms. The fragrance is, as usual, delightful. These grow from five to seven feet, and are so vigorous and disease resistant that they make fine "landscape plants."

THE CHINA ROSES

It is from these that the Hybrid Teas—and later the Floribundas and Grandifloras—got their free-blooming character. They are, perhaps, of greater historical than garden interest. There are two early Chinas, the Pink and the Red. The former is more vigorous, to five or six feet in a few years, while the more slender-caned Red will take years to reach five feet. The blooms are "loosely double," and have a more delicate texture of petals than the roses discussed up to now. They are not as hardy as most of the other groups—where 0 degrees F. is usual in winter they must have ample protection. A full disease protection program is a must as well. The Chinas differ from most other roses in that the blooms grow darker as they mature in the sun, instead of bleaching. Pinks turn quite deep red and whites take on pink tones of varying intensity.

The best approximation of the original Pink is variously called Old Blush China, Pink China, or Old Pink Daily. The large clusters of carmine-rose buds open a real *blush* pink—if such a thing as a blush still exists.

The Red is harder to come by, as there are a number of different kinds masquerading under the name Red China or even Slater's Crimson China.

Either of these can be grown—with protection—as far north as Long Island, but they do not really develop well except in very mild climates. The twiggy plants of the Red have few, but nasty, thorns, and the wood is dark, unlike the green canes and twigs of the Pink kinds. The Red, naturally, has red blooms, which are sparingly double and are more often borne singly than in clusters of three.

SOME GOOD HYBRIDS

CRAMOISI SUPERIEUR

The red color is deeper than that of Red China, but it has weak necks, which some like—but I don't. Yet, in all honesty, it makes a great mass of color in the garden for months on end, so you might give it a try.

FABVIER

There are those who list this as a China—maybe it is—but it only grows ten to twelve inches high, so it would seem to belong to the Miniatures, many of which have much China breeding. In any case, it has white stripes on bright crimson petals, with small blooms and good repeating.

KING GEORGE

The dark, velvety crimson blooms are fragrant and repeat very well. This has long been grown (1820), but is seldom seen now. A pity!

GRUSS AN TEPLITZ

Just where this belongs is debatable, but some place it here. If this is right, we have to adjust some of our concepts of at least this member of the group. As a beginning gardener, just short of my teens (too long ago to think about!) I grew this in southern New Hampshire, at our second summer place. We arrived in mid-June and left on Labor Day. No winter protection, no care until blooming time, and not too much then. This delightful rose was my pride and joy. Countless rich, velvety red, semi-double blooms with a central "boss" of bright yellow stamens appeared on the twiggy, 18-inch plants all summer long. In milder climates it will be larger. It may take some searching to find it today, but it is worth it.

THE TEA ROSES

There are more of the old Teas than old Chinas in gardens—where they are hardy. And with good reason. They bloom and bloom and bloom, certainly, and they are fragrant and have a delicate, thin-textured, graceful charm no other group can surpass. They get black spot, but while it doesn't seem to bother them, they thus become a source of infection for other roses, so should be sprayed. Mildew I have never seen on them. The few I have now survived decades of neglect before I bought the property, and some more since. They are always the last to be quelled by frost.

There are some cultivars that are hardier than others, but to be on the safe side, if temperatures usually fall below 10 degrees F., give some protection. Pruning should be on the *light* side.

SOME OF THE BEST

A large number of Teas are still being grown, but not that many in this country. Still, we do have domestic sources for a good number, and some of the best of them are listed below.

CATHERINE MERMET

Hardy to only about 15 degrees F., she produces medium-small blooms of exquisite form, colored soft pink with creamy overtones. Wonderfully fragrant.

DUCHESS DE BRABANT

She isn't any hardier, but bears soft, "luminescent-pink" blooms constantly. These blooms are cup shaped and very fragrant, with the real "tea scent." In cool weather the color deepens. The plant usually stops at four feet.

MAMAN COCHET

"Mama" has always been a favorite—with her large, heavily perfumed, and perfectly formed blooms, even if the substance is quite thin. The problem is to describe the color—it normally is a creamy white with an overlay of soft pink—but in cooler weather the pink gains considerable intensity. There is a worthwhile white form, too.

ROSETTE DELIZY

This is a good yellow with red on the petal tips. It blooms continuously, and is delightfully fragrant. The plant grows to four feet and has no disease problems.

SAFRANO

This is among the first of the Teas of high quality that appeared shortly after the introduction of the first Teas and Chinas about 1800. It is a large plant, to six feet. The fairly large, cupped blooms are either bold or soft yellow, depending on the climate, but always repeat faithfully and are wonderfully fragrant.

THE HARDIER ONES

Some of the hardier cultivars might well be in the above list, but they should be the first tried by those whose climate is less than ideal. Start with some of these: Safrano, Marie van Houtte (deep cream-white), Harry Kirk, Mrs. Dudley Cross, and William R. Smith. These can go to the southern shores of Long Island, or with good protection, to sheltered spots on Cape Cod.

CLIMBING TEAS

There are a number of fine cultivars in this group—but they are not easy to come by. They have the same recurrent bloom, the classic form, the same thin substance, and the wonderful fragrance of the bush types. They are, of course, even more tender than the bush forms.

GLOIRE DE DIJON

This one is big! It will grow to twenty feet and repeatedly bear fragrant flowers whose color is a blend of salmon, orange, and pink.

REVEIL DIJONAIS

The blooms are cerise with yellow in the center, on a strong plant.

SOMBREUIL

The least vigorous of the group, suitable as a Pillar, this cultivar has blooms that are fully double, perfectly formed, fragrant, and cream colored.

THE BOURBON ROSES

Some Bourbon roses played an influential part in the development of the Hybrid Perpetuals, but today they are seldom seen. This is too bad, for there are a number of really nice things here, and they should not be lost.

As a group they are compact and vigorous shrubs with green canes and large, very glossy, bright green leaves that show some purple shadings. Most repeat rather sparingly, but the fall blooms are of better quality than those produced in summer. Unless another height is noted, they grow from four to six feet.

SOME GOOD ONES

HERMOSA 7.8

No other Bourbon repeats as constantly as this. The cupped blooms are mauve-pink. A beauty!

HONORINE DE BRABANT 7.3

The big, deep, and beautifully quartered flowers are amazing in that there are seldom two the same. The base color varies from blush to white, over which are mottled areas and stripes of mauve and violet. The fragrance is nice, too.

LA REINE VICTORIA

A number of Bourbons mutate, giving two almost identical cultivars with different-colored blooms. La Reine has deep rose-pink blooms with a strong fragrance. These are wonderful for cutting as they last amazingly well. A sport from this has soft, flesh-pink blooms, and is named Madame Pierre Oger.

MADAME ISAAC PEREIRE 8.0

Here we have a similar case. The blooms of this are intensely fragrant, fully doubled, and quartered. The color is a rich, reddish-pink. When she mutated, Madame Ernest Calvat, which has rich pink blooms, was produced.

SOUVENIR DE LA MALMAISON 7.1

This is the most famous Bourbon of them all—and also the smallest, at three to four feet. It repeats almost constantly with wonderfully fragrant, large, flesh-colored blooms, which sometimes have deeper pink in the center. There is said to be a climbing form, but I can't find it.

VARIEGATA DI BOLOGNA 7.8

Here is a big one—to eight feet. The large, very double flowers are white, striped magenta and purple—in clear bands, not like Honorine de Brabant. The very fragrant blooms are borne in small clusters, mainly during a long summer season, but a few blooms show in the fall.

ZEPHERINE DROUHIN 7.9

And here we have another eight-footer—which repeats much better. The delightful, delicate fragrance comes from big, bright-pink flowers that are less double than most Bourbons. The canes have no thorns. This has sported, too, giving us Kathleen Harrop, which has shell-pink blooms on a less vigorous plant up to five feet or so.

Jan. 93 - Germston

/Heritage - Pink · soft · Fragrant ⎫ all English Roses
Mary Rose - Pink · deeper " ⎭

Legend - Red ⅋ Tea Rose

Appendixes
and
Bibliography

Appendix 1

Rose Organizations

There are two rose organizations in the United States that are important to all who grow roses, commercially or as amateurs.

ALL-AMERICA ROSE SELECTIONS

Only commercial growers and breeders can be part of this group. It maintains rose test gardens at 21 widely different locations and tests roses, for two years, before they are introduced. The member firms supply the plants for these tests. When the data are in, they arrange to have them evaluated. One (or more) of the top-rated cultivars is named All-American Rose Selection (AARS) of the following year, when it (or they) will be introduced.

While it is not meant to claim that only AARS roses are good, it does say that those which bear the seal are widely adaptable and of superior quality, having made superior scores in a wide variety of climates and soils.

Recently, the base of the testing has been widened from the former three major classes—Hybrid Teas, Floribundas, and Grandifloras. Now Shrubs and some other types have a place in the program; this is all to the good.

Publicity on the winners, as well as general information on their culture, is supplied to garden writers and the media in general. High-class art work is also included. There is no charge for this.

AMERICAN ROSE SOCIETY

Membership in the society carries benefits for amateurs and professionals alike. Membership is worldwide. Each member receives 12 issues of *The American Rose* (magazine), a copy of *The American Rose Annual* (a 260-page book), and, on request, the society's *A Handbook for Selecting Roses*.

A major item in every annual is the section called "The Proof of the Pudding." Here the more recent rose cultivars are rated, on a scale of one to ten, by members in various parts of the country as well as some test gardens. Very generally, such ratings are much more reliable than the advertising blurbs of some catalog writers. In other words, this can save you money!

The society has a good library of rose books. Members can borrow these, either in person or by mail.

Where cultural problems are encountered, the society stands ready to help, either from headquarters or through Consulting Rosarians, located in every part of the country.

Two national conventions are held each year, in conjunction with the National Rose Show—where the major regional and national trophies are awarded.

A list is available that tells of members' gardens that are open for visits—in almost every section of the country.

At present (1973) the annual dues are $10.50.

Work has just been completed on a new headquarters building and major display garden, on a 118-acre site near Shreveport, Louisiana. The management of the society will move there early in 1974.

Appendix 2

Rose Display and Test Gardens

All too many people think of the fine and often large rose display gardens as places where they can spend an afternoon, or even a whole day, just drinking in the color and perfume. This is a most enjoyable thing to do. On the other hand, such gardens have a far greater potential than that. They provide places where you can compare the different kinds and cultivars against your own likes and dislikes. You can pick up information on rose culture, not only when the plants are in bloom, but especially when the plants are ready for winter.

In the test sections, of course, it is like a fashion show. You can see what new items you will want for your own.

A couple of years ago there were estimated to be about 130 municipal rose gardens, with many other display gardens, spread over the country. Make it a point to see as many as you can, year after year. You'll have some good times and—perhaps more important—learn a lot.

In the following lists, an asterisk (*) means that there is a test section for the AARS.

CALIFORNIA

Arcadia: Arcadia County Rose Garden
Berkeley: Berkeley Rose Garden
Fresno: Fresno Municipal Rose Garden
Hemet: Howard Rose Company*
La Canada: Descanso Gardens
Los Angeles: Exposition Park Rose Garden
Oakland: Oakland Municipal Rose Garden
Ontario: Armstrong Nurseries*
Riverside: White Park Rose Garden
Sacramento: State Capital Grounds Rose Garden
San Jose: San Jose Municipal Rose Garden; Stocking Rose Nursery*
San Marino: Huntington Botanical Garden
Santa Barbara: Santa Barbara Memorial Rose Garden
Tulare: Visalia Garden Club Rose Garden
Tustin: Jackson and Perkins Company Test Garden*
Wasco: Wasco Rose Garden

COLORADO

Denver: Denver Botanic Garden*
Littleton: War Memorial Rose Garden

CONNECTICUT

Hartford: Elizabeth Park Rose Garden

FLORIDA

Gainesville: Cecil Mathews Memorial Rose Garden
Miami: Stanley Mott Nursery

GEORGIA

Atlanta: Greater Atlanta Rose Garden
Pine Mountain (Chipley): Ida Cason Calloway Gardens
Savannah: Memorial Hospital Rose Garden
Thomasville: Thomasville Nurseries (a fine source of old and tender cultivars)

IDAHO

Boise: Municipal Rose Garden
Pocatello: Rotary Rose Garden

ILLINOIS

Chicago: Grant Park Rose Garden; Washington Park Rose Garden
Highland Park: Gardeners' Memorial Garden
Sheator: Sheator Municipal Rose Garden
Waukegan: Diamond Rose Garden

INDIANA

Fort Wayne: Lakeside Rose Garden
Richmond: E. G. Hill Memorial Rose Garden

IOWA

> Ames: Iowa State University, Department of Horticulture*
> Davenport: Municipal Rose Garden
> Sioux City: Grandview Park Rose Garden

KANSAS

> Hays: Fort Hays Garden Club, at Fort Hays State College
> Manhattan: Kansas State University Rose Garden
> Topeka: Reinish Rose and Test Garden

LOUISIANA

> Lafayette: University of Southwest Louisiana Test Garden*
> New Orleans: Municipal Rose Gardens

MASSACHUSETTS

> Boston: Fenway Rose Garden; Franklin Park Rose Garden

MICHIGAN

> East Lansing: Michigan State University Horticultural Gardens
> Lansing: Cooley Gardens

MINNESOTA

> Duluth: Duluth Rose Garden
> Minneapolis: Municipal Rose Garden*
> Winona: Memorial Rose Garden

MISSISSIPPI

Jackson: Jackson Municipal Rose Garden

MISSOURI

Cape Giraudeau: Cape Giraudeau Rose Display Garden
Kansas City: Municipal Rose Garden
St. Louis: Missouri Botanical (Shaw) Garden; Jewel Box Rose Garden
(Forest Park)

MONTANA

Missoula: Memorial Rose Garden

NEVADA

Reno: Reno Memorial Rose Garden

NEW JERSEY

Freehold: Bobbink Nurseries, Inc.*

NEW MEXICO

Hobbs: Community Rose Garden

NEW YORK

Bronx: New York Botanical Garden
Brooklyn: Brooklyn Botanic Garden
Buffalo: Niagara Frontier Trial Rose Garden

Farmingdale: State University, Agricultural and Technical College*
Ithaca: Cornell University Rose Garden
Rochester: Municipal Rose Garden
Syracuse: Dr. E. M. Mills Municipal Rose Garden

NORTH CAROLINA

Asheville: Biltmore House Rose Garden
Charlotte: Charlotte Municipal Rose Garden (Independence Park)
Raleigh: Raleigh Municipal Rose Garden

OHIO

Akron: Memorial Rose Garden
Columbus: Park of Roses
            Ohio State University, Department of Horticulture*
Lorain: Lakeview Park Rose Garden
Mansfield: Kingwood Center
Mentor: Melvin Wyant Rose Garden
Wooster: Garden of Roses of Legend and Romance at the Ohio Agricultural
        Research and Development Center (Old roses)
Youngstown: Fellows Riverside Garden (Mill Creek Park)

OKLAHOMA

Bartlesville: Johnson Park Municipal Rose Garden
Norman: Norman Memorial Rose Garden
Oklahoma City: Municipal Rose Garden

Tulsa: Woodward Park Greenhouse*
Woodward: Woodward Rose Garden

OREGON

Eugene: Owen Park Municipal Rose Garden
Portland: International Rose Test Garden*
          Lewis and Clark Memorial Rose Garden

PENNSYLVANIA

Allentown: M. W. Gross Memorial Rose Garden
Hershey: Hershey Rose Garden
Kennett Square: Longwood Gardens
Lancaster: Fritz Memorial Rose Garden
Philadelphia: Morris Arboretum (Chestnut Hill); Philadelphia Zoological
          Society Rose Garden
Pittsburgh: Mellon Park Rose Garden (Schenley Park)
Pottstown: Pottstown Municipal Rose Garden
Reading: Reading Municipal Rose Garden
University Park: Pennsylvania State University Rose Garden
West Grove: Conard-Pyle Company*
Williamsport: Williamsport Municipal Rose Garden

RHODE ISLAND

Barrington: Llys-Yr-Rhosyn (93 Rumstick Road)

SOUTH CAROLINA

> Florence: Timrod Park Rose Garden
> Greenville: Cleveland Park Rose Garden; Furman University Rose Garden
> Orangeburg: Edisto Gardens*
> Parr: Fairfield County Memorial Hospital Rose Garden

TENNESSEE

> Chattanooga: Municipal Rose Garden
> Memphis: Memphis Memorial Rose Garden

TEXAS

> Amarillo: Memorial Park Rose Garden
> Corpus Christi: Corpus Christi Rose Society Test Garden (Hewitt Estates Park)
> Dallas: Dallas Garden Center (Fair Park)
>   Samuell-Grand Municipal Rose Garden
> El Paso: Municipal Rose Garden
> Fort Worth: Fort Worth Botanic Garden
> San Antonio: Jefferson Gardens
> Tyler: Municipal Rose Garden Park*

UTAH

> Fillmore: State House Museum Trial Garden
> Nephi: Municipal Memorial Rose Garden
> Provo: Provo Municipal Rose Garden
> Salt Lake City: Salt Lake Municipal Rose Garden

Virginia

Arlington: Arlington Memorial Rose Garden (Arlington Hospital)
Roanoke: Mountain View Fishburn Garden

Washington

Aberdeen: Aberdeen Municipal Rose Garden (Benn Park)
Bellingham: Cornwall Park Rose Garden; Fairhaven Park Rose Garden
Chehalis: Chehalis Municipal Rose Garden; Evergreen Rose Garden
Seattle: Woodland Park Rose Garden
Spokane: Rose Hill (Manito Park)
Tacoma: Point Defiance Park Rose Garden

Wisconsin

Hale's Corners: Boerner Botanical Gardens (Whitnall Park)

Appendix 3

Sources of Plants and Materials

MINIATURE ROSES

A great number of sources are available for Miniature Roses, but these are among the tops, with a greater number of cultivars available than most:

Conard-Pyle Company, West Grove, Pa. 19390
Mini-Roses, P.O. Box 4255, Station A, Dallas, Tex. 75208
Sequoia Nurseries, 2519 East Noble, Visalia, Calif. 93277
Spring Hill Nurseries, Tipp City, Ohio 45371
Wayside Gardens, Mentor, Ohio 44060
Wyant's Roses, Mentor, Ohio 44060

TREE ROSES

Armstrong Nurseries, Inc., Ontario, Calif. 91761
Conard-Pyle Company, West Grove, Pa. 19390

Jackson and Perkins Company, Medford, Ore. 97501
Sequoia Nurseries (for Miniature Trees), 2519 East Noble, Visalia, Calif. 93277
Stocking Rose Nursery, 12505 North Capital Avenue, San Jose, Calif. 95133

OLD ROSES

Joseph J. Kern, Box 33, Mentor, Ohio 44060
Tillotson's Roses, Brown's Valley Road, Watsonville, Calif. 95076
Thomasville Nurseries, Inc., Thomasville, Ga. 31792
Wayside Gardens, Mentor, Ohio 44060
Wyant's Roses, Mentor, Ohio 44060

"HARD-TO-FIND" CULTIVARS

Joseph J. Kern, Box 33, Mentor, Ohio 44060
Roses By Fred Edmunds, P.O. Box 68, Wilsonville, Ore. 97070
Stern's Nursery, Inc., Geneva, N.Y. 14456 (Sub-Zero Hybrid Teas)
Tillotson's Roses, Brown's Valley Road, Watsonville, Calif. 95076
Wayside Gardens, Mentor, Ohio 44060
Wyant's Roses, Mentor, Ohio 44060

TOOLS AND SUPPLIES

American Standard Company, 1 West Street, Plantsville, Conn. 06479 (Florian Ratchet-Cut pruning tools)
F & R Farrell Company, 6810 Biggert Road, London, Ohio 43140 (winter protection materials)

H. D. Hudson Manufacturing Company, 154 East Erie Street, Chicago, Ill. 60611 ("Ladybug sprayers"—a wide range of sprayers and dusters)

Root-Lowell, Lowell, Mich. 49331 (Atomist 1026 and 1027—a wide range of sprayers and dusters)

Roses By Fred Edmunds, P.O. Box 68, Wilsonville, Ore. 97070 (Felco pruners and gardeners' gloves)

MICROPOROUS PIPE

International Plastics, Inc., Colwich, Kans. 67030

MOLE EXTERMINATOR

Redco and Associates, Inc., P.O. Box 8283, Peoria, Ill. 61614

Appendix 4

The Best Roses for Hips

The average rose grower who confines himself to Hybrid Teas, Floribundas, and Grandifloras, with possibly a Climber or two, never sees a rose bush in fruit. This is too bad, as the hips may be colorful, last long into the winter in some instances, and even be a source of good food. They can also be a good source of bird food, thus keeping our friends nearby.

Once-blooming roses should be pruned with this in mind. Recurrent-blooming kinds must have faded flowers removed to prevent the formation of the hips, in order to produce the greatest possible bloom. But there are some, especially *R. rugosa*, which will produce blooms and hips side by side during the latter part of the season.

For our purposes, however, all kinds that produce hips are not necessarily good. The Scotch rose, *R. spinosissima*, and many derived from it, have lots of hips, but they are small and black, with little attractiveness.

The forms of the hips vary widely—as does size. Small, berrylike hips are of ornamental value only if they are produced in large numbers and have an attractive color. Long urn-shaped hips, as with *R. moyesii* and its cultivars, are outstanding. The large, bulbous hips of *R. rugosa* look like the spires of a Russian Orthodox church and are "lacquer red"—a lovely sight! They are also good to eat, as are many others large enough to make the picking worthwhile. In seaside areas where *R. rugosa* has become naturalized, considerable quantities can be scavenged.

Try some of these:

Rosa alba semiplena

R. blanda

R. canina and cultivars

R. glutinosa

R. macrantha

R. moschata and cultivars

R. moyesii and cultivars

R. nitida

R. pomifera

R. roxburghii

R. rubrifolia

R. rugosa and cultivars

R. virginiana

R. wichuraiana, Max Graf and some of the Brownell Ground-Cover Series

Appendix 5

Importing Roses

What used to be a long-drawn-out and chancy business has been radically eased— by air freight.

Rose growers who get deeply involved, especially in species, Shrub and Old roses, often find that what they want is not available in this country.

The first step is to check Canadian catalogs, for there is no red tape in importing from our neighbor.

If this leads to a blank wall, try other countries. Don't try Australia, New Zealand, Italy, or the Republic of South Africa, however, for roses may not be imported from them. England, France, and West Germany will be your best bets.

Importing from these countries is not difficult. As soon as you get the catalog, act quickly, to be certain that when you get your order in the kinds you want are still in stock.

Write the Permit Section, Plant Importation Branch, U.S. Department of Agriculture, 209 River Street, Hoboken, N.J. 07030. They will send you a form to fill out, describing the kinds and numbers of plants you wish to import, and from whom.

You will be required to keep these plants isolated under "post-entry quarantine" for two years. This must be in an area accessible to state inspectors whenever required.

When the permit is issued, you can order your roses, including the permit with the order.

Insist on delivery by air. Losses in surface delivery can be staggering.

The plants will be delivered to Hoboken, inspected, treated only if necessary, repackaged, and delivered to you. Now this usually takes about two weeks—as against many weeks previously.

The minimal red tape is a refreshing change from some governmental procedures!

Appendix 6

Rose Recipes

RUGOSA ROSE JAM

Wash 2 cups of hips and cut out the calyx from each. Cook in 2 cups of water, mashing until tender. Put through a fine sieve to remove the seeds. Cook the pulp with an equal amount of sugar until it reaches jam consistency. Pour into a jar and seal.

ROSE HIP SYRUP

An excellent source of vitamin C.

Wash 2 pounds of hips, cover with water, bring to a boil, and simmer until soft. Put into a jelly bag and squeeze out the juice. Return the pulp to the pan, add water, and simmer again. Squeeze the juice. Add a pound of sugar to the juice, bring to a boil and stir for 5 minutes. Bottle and seal while hot.

ROSE SYRUP

This recipe was furnished to the All-America Rose Selection's "Rose News" by Jean Hersey, Tryon, North Carolina. It is excellent for adding the rose flavor to cookies, fondant, and icings.

Gather half a dozen fragrant red roses and clean off all spray residue. Remove the petals and cut off the slightly bitter base of each. Simmer the petals, covered, for about 30 minutes in a small amount of water and ½ cup brown sugar. When strained, the result will make 1½ tall glasses of syrup, which looks like wine and tastes "the way roses smell."

POTPOURRI

A properly made potpourri, when stored in a tight jar, will hold its fragrance for years.

It would seem that no two people make their potpourris alike. Some people even make theirs differently from time to time—to develop different fragrances.

THE PETALS

Only the most fragrant roses should be used. The time of harvest is important. Pick the blooms midway between first opening and full bloom. Pick in the morning, just as soon as the dew has gone and they are perfectly dry. Pull the petals and lay them on cheesecloth or clean paper in an airy, dry, and warm room away from sunlight. Where large numbers are to be dried, try supporting a screen door between two kitchen chairs or stools; they will dry from the top and bottom at the same time.

A SIMPLE RECIPE

Although many recipes are very involved, a simple one can give very good results. For each quart of dried petals add a couple of teaspoons of a fixative—usually powdered orris root or gum benzoin. These may be purchased from your druggist. Mix the fixative with a tablespoon of spices—one or more of the following: cinnamon, allspice, clove, or nutmeg.

Mix this with the petals, pack in a jar or crock, and seal tightly. Stir from time to time. Proper aging takes from six to eight weeks.

If, during the aging period, the mix should feel damp, stir in a cup of salt to prevent mold.

OTHER INGREDIENTS

The fragrant leaves and flowers of other plants can be added at will, usually about a cupful per quart of rose petals. Some of the ones commonly used are lavender, lemon verbena, thyme (especially the lemon-scented one), the sweetest of carnations and garden pinks, orange blossoms, rosemary, scented geranium leaves, and even a bay leaf or two.

An orange skin, grated and dried, adds a sweet note, while lemon skin gives one less sweet.

A ROSE JAR

For one quart of dried rose petals:

Pound (grind) $\frac{1}{2}$ pound bay salt, then add 1 pound kitchen salt. Mix $\frac{2}{3}$ teaspoon each of nutmeg, allspice, and cloves. Add $\frac{3}{4}$ ounce orris root and $\frac{1}{2}$ ounce storax. Mix all of these thoroughly. Put a layer in the bottom of a rose jar, then add a layer of rose petals. Repeat until all the materials are used. Seal the jar tightly. Every once in a while, during the first couple of months, reach into the jar with a long fork and stir well.

A MOIST POTPOURRI

This is a good kind to make if you don't have many petals available at one time. Also, it will have a stronger fragrance than a dry one.

Make a layer of fresh petals in the bottom of the jar and sprinkle with salt — use enough so no mold develops. Repeat as more petals are available, adding lavender and other flower petals from time to time. Keep the jar tightly sealed between additions. When the jar is about full, add some grated and dried orange or lemon peel, a tablespoon of ground cloves, and some allspice. Mix from time to time during the first couple of months. The fragrance should get stronger as time goes on.

CONTAINERS

If you have enough petals to make large batches in a season, large crocks are convenient for the making and aging. When the product has aged enough, it can be put into smaller, ornamental jars. The easiest kind to find is a ginger jar, many of which have lovely designs on them, usually with a Chinese motif. The true potpourri jars are best, but they are hard to locate. These look like ginger jars but have two covers, an outer one, which makes a tight seal, and an inner one, which is perforated, and which releases the fragrance when the outer cap is removed.

Some potpourri makers like to bottle theirs in clear glass jars, especially apothecary jars. When this is done, add some petals of delphinium and other colorful flowers to add interest. Avoid mums and marigolds, as their odors are not pleasant. Small sprigs of lacy foliage, including ferns, can be glued to the inside of the jar before it is filled.

However you package your potpourris, they make lovely gifts for any occasion.

Cecil Brunner Climb. On Cloth. Line
" " Bush - behind Orchids
" " " - Back new wall

Double Delight - Back Yard - Rose garden
" Fence over Orchids
" Side yard

? - Pretty Salmon Climb. - On back Wall Fence - Was Kates from old home

Queen Elizabeth Climb. N. Side of garge.

Bibliography

A BEGINNING LIST

A long, detailed bibliography, no matter how scholarly, can scare a beginner to death. Because of this, here are three rose books which, I believe, will be most helpful:

ALLEN, R. C. *Roses for Every Garden.* New York: M. Barrows and Company, 1948. Dr. Allen is a former executive secretary of the American Rose Society. His book is sound on culture, lucid, and a joy to read.

THOMSON, RICHARD, and WILSON, HELEN VAN PELT. *Roses for Pleasure.* Princeton, N.J.: D. Van Nostrand Company, Inc., 1957. Uncomplicated, sound culture based on personal experience and lightened with real enthusiasm. The sections on the Old roses are especially good.

WESCOTT, DR. CYNTHIA. *Anyone Can Grow Roses*. New York: The Macmillan Company, 1967. Be sure to get the latest edition, as this is periodically updated. A milestone in rose literature—nothing less! As the "Plant Doctor," she cared for thousands of her clients' roses for many years, as well as growing her own. The distilled knowledge from all of this is simply and enthusiastically stated. (N.B. Don't let the frighteningly long list of rose troubles make you pessimistic —she is a top plant pathologist, so is clinically technical in this one area.)

WIDENING THE HORIZONS

As we gain experience—and enthusiasm—we tend to go further and further for our information and even just reading pleasure. Here are some avenues you can take.

MOORE, RALPH S. *All About Miniature Roses*. Kansas City, Mo.: Diversity Books, 1966. As one of the top breeders of Miniature roses, Ralph knows whereof he speaks—and he speaks easily and well.

ROCKWELL, F. F., and GRAYSON, ESTHER C. *The Rockwells' Complete Book of Roses*. Garden City, N.Y.: Doubleday and Company, Inc., 1958. Based on long and varied experience.

SHEPHERD, ROY E. *The History of the Rose*. New York: The Macmillan Company, 1954. An astounding piece of work—an absolute must for students of the Old roses.

THOMAS, GRAHAM STUART. *The Old Shrub Roses* [English]. Boston: Charles T. Branford Company, 1957. Universally admired.

THOMSON, RICHARD. *Old Roses for Modern Gardens*. Princeton, N.J.: D. Van Nostrand Company, Inc., 1959. Perceptive and enthusiastic discussions of some of the many hundreds of kinds he has grown. A must in the field.

WILSON, HELEN VAN PELT. *Climbing Roses*. New York: M. Barrows and Company, Inc., 1955. A rather neglected group is treated with perception and affection.

COON, NELSON. *Fragrance and Fragrant Plants for House and Garden*. Grandview, Mo.: Diversity Books, 1967. Besides going into the nature of fragrance, Mr. Coon has a chapter on rose fragrance and one on potpourris. Once you get that far, you won't stop there—any more than with the next two titles.

RHODE, ELEANOR SINCLAIR. *The Scented Garden*. Boston: Hale, Cushman and Flint, 1936. Long a standard, very fine. Potpourris and other recipes are included here, too.

WILSON, HELEN VAN PELT, and BELL, LEONIE. *The Fragrant Year*. M. Barrows and Company, Inc., 1967. Distributed by William Morrow and Company, New York. Two gifted gardeners have produced a scholarly work—but don't be put off by that. It is written in infectiously enthusiastic prose with a precision of description—in a notably imprecise field—I once thought impossible. The illustrations by Mrs. Bell are, as usual, beautiful and horticulturally accurate as well. The list of roses discussed is unbelievably long and complete. Potpourris are included here, too.

GORDON, JEAN. *The Art of Cooking with Roses*. New York: Walker and Company,

1968. Besides foods, there are recipes for lotions, potpourris, and other interesting things.

―――. *Pageant of the Rose.* New York: Studio Publications, Inc., in association with Thomas Y. Crowell Company, 1953. A beautifully made book treating legends, history, art, cooking, etc., etc., etc. A classic.

PERIODICALS

The American Rose (magazine), published monthly by the American Rose Society, 4048 Roselea Place, Columbus, Ohio 43214 (after February, 1974, at P.O. Box 30,000, Shreveport, La. 71130). All members receive it.

The American Rose Annual, 1916–   . The American Rose Society. All members receive it.

A Handbook for Selecting Roses, issued annually by the American Rose Society. Free to all members, on request; the cost to others is ten cents and a self-addressed, stamped envelope. Gives the latest ratings and some descriptive material on a large number of cultivars.

Index

-N-

Back Yard Wall

x Climber - Kate's rose

x Fragrant Cloud

x Cecil Brunner

Queen Elizabet x   Fragrant Cloud
x   x

Double Delight   x D.D.
x

x Bridal Pink   x Ice Berg wt.

x Pink   x Dainty Bliss - Pink

x Mon Cheri
Crimson/Red

Single Old
x Wilhelm Red
Creen - single old
x?

Patio

Cecil Brunner
x

Dowell D. ← + + x Red + 3 Pink Ulterion Rose

Center

x min   Close Line
Cecil Brunner Climber

x Climber
white small clusters
Irish - No thorns

x Rose-d-or
apricot little

Shack

x Charlotte Armstrong

Side Yard
-E-

x Mr Lincoln   x Show Boy

? Lavender
x

x Red   x Alea

x D.D   x Dad. O   x Sweet Surender

Garage
Brick Wall
x
Queen Elizabeth Climber
on wall.

House
x
English . (Mary Rose)
Raw PINK

Mini Tree - Summer Beuter (near Cherry Tree) Pot
2 Trees (ft. step) - Show Boy

PHOTO CREDITS

Color:

Plate I: Valley Studios, courtesy of Howard's of Hemet, California
Plates II, III: George Taloumis
Plates IV, V: Stemler, courtesy of Will Tillotson's Roses
Plate VI: courtesy of Howard's of Hemet, California
Plate VII: courtesy of Conard-Pyle

Plate VIII: courtesy of Longwood Gardens

Black-and-white:

Page 5: courtesy of Longwood Gardens
Pages 12, 19, 20, 27, 41, 89, 91, 92, 94, 118, 129, 132, 151: Paul E. Genereux

Pages 53, 54, 62: courtesy of All-American Rose Selection (AARS)
Page 77: courtesy of Howards of Hemet, California
Pages 81, 139, 145, 148, 164, 168, 189, 195: George Taloumis
Pages 159, 173, 176, 179, 186, 192, 201: Stemler, courtesy of Will Tillotson's Roses

Fred J. Nisbet was born in Cambridge, Massachusetts, in 1912, took his B.S. in landscape architecture at the University of Massachusetts in 1934, and worked in various nurseries in Massachusetts and Connecticut before taking his Ph.D. in ornamental horticulture at Cornell in 1949. From 1949 to 1952 he was assistant professor of ornamental horticulture at West Virginia University, where he founded the University Plantations and *West Virginia Nursery Notes.* He served as editor of publications for the American Rose Society, 1952–1956; as superintendent of the Biltmore Estate, Asheville, North Carolina, 1956–1962; as regional editor, *Flower and Garden Magazine,* 1958–1971; and as president, Southeastern Chapter, American Rhododendron Society, 1959–1961. Since 1963 he has been vice-president, Garden Treasures, Inc., Tryon, North Carolina. He has lectured widely, and is the author of more than a hundred articles in newspapers and trade and professional journals, as well as co-author of *The Golden Guide to Flowers* (1962).

A Note about the Type

The text of this book was set in a film version of Palatino, a type face designed by the noted German typographer Hermann Zapf. Named after Giovanbattista Palatino, a writing master of Renaissance Italy, Palatino was the first of Zapf's type faces to be introduced to America. The first designs for the face were made in 1948, and the fonts for the complete face were issued between 1950 and 1952. Like all Zapf-designed type faces, Palatino is beautifully balanced and exceedingly readable.

The book was composed by
University Graphics, Shrewsbury, New Jersey;
printed and bound by
The Halliday Lithograph Corporation, West Hanover, Massachusetts.

The typography and binding design are by
Earl Tidwell.